CHAR

The Eagle's Voice DESCRIBES

THR SOULS JOURNEY BACK
TO EARTHMAKER AND HOW
IN SOMB WAYS IT OPRATES
MR. ENJOY

Martin
4.15.01

The Eagle's Voice

Tales Told by Indian Effigy Mounds

Gary J. Maier, M.D.

PRAIRIE OAK PRESS
Madison, Wisconsin

First edition, first printing
Copyright © 2001 by Gary J. Maier, M.D.

Prairie Oak Press
821 Prospect Place
Madison, WI 53703

Cover designed by Flying Fish Graphics, Blue Mounds, Wisconsin
Printed in the United States of America on acid-free paper by
Sheridan Books, Chelsea, Michigan

Appendix B: Wisdom of the Oak, has been adapted from an article published in the *Waunakee Tribune,* 83:3, December 31, 1998.

Library of Congress Cataloging-in-Publication Data

Maier, Gary J.
 The Eagle's Voice : tales told by Indian effigy mounds /
Gary J. Maier.—1st ed.
    p.   cm.
Includes bibliographical references.
ISBN 1-879483-74-2 (pbk. : alk. paper)
  1. Mounds—Wisconsin—Mendota, Lake. 2. Indians of North America —Wisconsin—Mendota, Lake—Folklore. 3. Indians of North America—Wisconsin—Mendota, Lake—Antiquities. 4. Earthworks (Archaeology)—Wisconsin—Mendota, Lake. 5. Mendota, Lake (Wis.)—Antiquities. I. Title.

E78.W8 M35 2001
977.5'83—dc21   2001018553

I want to thank the Ho-Chunk for their patience, and for sharing these perennial thoughts of the new beginning that each life offers. Thanks to all my relatives, especially my parents, my sister, my children, and my grandchildren. To Sandy, my love, and friends who helped to bring me new perspectives on life. Finally, thanks to the inspiration of the Faith Community at the St. Benedict Center, Middleton.

CONTENTS

INTRODUCTION

There is a small convent on the Via Delorosa in Jerusalem that has in its basement, about 25 feet below the current street level, a road authenticated to be from Roman times, one that experts agree could very well be the one on which Christ walked on Good Friday, two thousand years ago. The nuns give brief tours to their basement and used to tell pilgrims that American tourists in particular wanted to see one of the rocks that Christ actually stepped on. Of course, this is impossible. But such is our hunger for historical, even spiritual certainty, that some cannot help but ask. What concerns the nuns is not that they cannot validate such a request, but that one has to leave such questions behind if one wants to move on the spiritual path. So the nuns now tell tour groups right at the beginning to "get your heads off the rocks."

As you go with me on my journey and hear part of my story, you will have to be prepared to "get your head off the rocks." It would be best if you could adopt such an attitude right at the beginning. But if you can't, then as we move along perhaps you will at some point realize that what's holding you back from "moving on" is a desire for factual certainty, one rooted in cultural and historical fact. While historical certainty is difficult to attain, cultural certainty can be discovered only if a knowledgeable member of the in-group shares the true meaning of the "facts." Without this, facts can only give us "information"—and at best point to something suspected but beyond verification. So, until Ho-Chunk and other Indian nations tell us the specific meaning of a mounds group, we can but make the first approximations in good faith.

Let us make another observation before we move on. The world appears in its simplest construction to be made of "matter." Matter has magically organized itself in some places into "living" or life forms. Life forms then appear, especially in humans, to have the capacity to think, and so we have entered the realm of mind. As a fourth progression, it appears to those inspired with greater wisdom that beyond the mind lies a realm called *spirit*. For more than ten thousand years, cultures around the world have buried their dead on the intuition, or experience, that some aspect of the person lives on beyond the grave. Matter-life-mind-spirit, a simple four-stage progression, is the core architecture of this perennial philosophy. Perhaps this simple continuum might act as a sort of ladder to lead us from the rock-bottom basement to the spiritual heights, since in our exploration we will start with the basic "matter" of a grave and then move beyond it, to what it might mean, and more.

In 1980 I discovered a figure describing about fifty effigy, conical, and linear mounds located on the northeast shore of Lake Mendota in Madison, Wisconsin. Stephen Peet, a Protestant minister, drew the figure around 1870 and published it in his book *Prehistoric America: The Mound Builders, Their Works and Relics*, in 1890. The mounds have since been divided into three groups. The western and middle groups are reasonably well preserved because they became part of the grounds of the state mental hospital, now called the Mendota Mental Health Institute. Those in the eastern group have been destroyed except for one eagle effigy mound that is now in the front yard of a house on the corner of Harper and Woodward Streets, in Madison. If you look at Figure 1, you will be able to pick out what appear to be five thunderbirds and three foxes in the eastern group, three eagles and a mound with a long curved tail called a "panther" representing the Water-Spirit Clan, in the middle group, and a number of conical mounds and long linear mounds in the western group. What follows is the journey I took with the help of Professor Jim Scherz, members of the Ancient Earth Work Society, the archives of the State Historical Society, and a turtle spirit, to understand the story these mounds tell when considered as earth writing.

Before we start the journey the reader should know that this is a work in progress. Appendix A describes more carefully the assumptions that I believe should underpin interpretive approaches to the mounds. It also expands the research started in this book giving the first application of the associations developed here by interpreting the story of the mounds at the Blackhawk Country Club, in Shorewood Hills, on the southwest shore of the lake. The similarities between these separate Lake Mendota mounds clusters, in my view, strengthens the conclusions of *The Eagle's Voice.* While Madison is the capital of the State of Wisconsin, given the distribution of the effigy mounds as described in Radin's book *The Winnebago Tribe*, it could be considered the effigy mounds capital of North America. While some would be critical of this perhaps romantic notion, there can little doubt that the mounds clusters around Lake Mendota mainly concerned the burial of important members of the Thunderbird, Eagle, Water-Spirit, and Bear clans. The Ho-Chunk named the lake *Wonk Shek Ho-Mikla*, that is, "place where the people (Indian people) died and are buried." Unfortunately, more than 80 percent of the approximately five thousand mounds that were constructed in the Madison area have been destroyed. On the other hand, the patterns and alignments found in the mounds that have survived, and are discussed here, are representative of patterns and alignments found in more than eighty other mounds groups. Because of erosion, specific features of some mounds have been lost and the exact alignment of others is subject to plus or minus one degree. Not withstanding this, the novel describes alignments as though they are exact. Finally, while equinox and solstice points on the horizon have had almost no variation over millennia, the heavenly constellations not only rotate around the place in the sky where the polar star, Polaris, rests, in one year, over the centuries the stars have moved among themselves, making an exact alignment to a known constellation dependent on knowing the historical time the mounds were constructed. Research in this area has been enhanced by the use of computer programs that can accurately regress the stars to their relative positions at any time in the past. Of value to this work then, has been the publication of a book, *Lakota Star Knowledge, Studies in Lakota Stellar Theology*, by Ronald Goodman, which describes nine constellations of the Sioux that may be relevant to these mounds.

Look at Figure 1 and consider that there were once more than a hundred groups of effigy mounds in Wisconsin alone, and they all told tales. They told stories about death, about battle, about leadership and other issues important to the culture. Then consider that this is a story of my personal journey through the mounds. The first two chapters are my imaginative reconstruction of past events that took place, at least in metaphor. I leave it to the reader to assess how well I have reconstructed them to fit our story. Chapters Three to Nine then describe in as factual manner as I can the development of a more than basic understanding of the mounds on the grounds of the Institute. But the notes and suggested readings are not meant to document the facts in scholarly fashion. Rather, they are meant to help amplify sentiments, notions, and interpretations, the place that your mind and spirit will want to go when no longer "stuck to the rocks." And since the world is change, don't be surprised if the Ho-Chunk, who used to be called the Winnebago, appear in costumes that never were. Come, then, on a journey that will teach you about the language system of the mounds. If you keep an open mind, perhaps you will learn something about yourself.

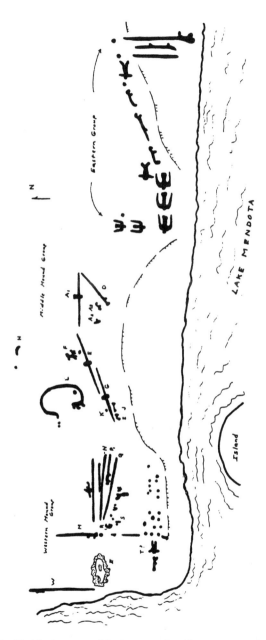

Figure 1. Dr. DeHarte was able to examine these mounds first hand because they were still intact. The Eastern Group were progressively destroyed in the early 1900s.

Prologue

VOICES

If we were logical, the future would be bleak indeed. But we are more than logical. We are human beings, and we have faith, and we have hope, and we can work.[1]

— Jacques Cousteau

The last of the human freedoms is to choose one's attitudes.

— Victor Frankl

The story that follows is a product of my life. The relevant parts started, however, in September of 1978 when I moved to Madison, Wisconsin. The story is in progress, but it is complete enough to share what are more than preliminary findings. Furthermore, the main thrust of this story is a "white man's" attempt to understand Native American cultures by presenting some of their monuments as evidence that the image that Euro-Americans have of their cultures is distorted and demeaning. It is my hope that after reading this story you will reexamine your attitude toward Native Americans.

While my personal story will not be told here because it is not the important one, the part of it that is shared followed the path of the medicine wheel. In 1978, I married. In 1988, my wife and I separated. In 1990, we divorced. Since then we have maintained a reasonable relationship as we have raised two wonderful girls, Liz and Sara. In the metaphor of the four directions of the medicine wheel, which is presented later in this story, you will note that from 1978 to 1988 I proceeded from a certain innocence in the South towards the darkness of the West. It would not be truthful to say that I did not black out. The fact that I was involved in understanding another aspect of Native Americans on my personal journey will have to wait for another book. Suffice it to say that on the other side of darkness lies wisdom and the beginning of illumination. These are the principal concepts of the North and the East. Innocence, introspection, wisdom, and illumination, the lessons to be learned in the place of each cardinal direction came alive as I have been privileged on my personal journey to rediscover and rework the Christian and pre-Christian roots that lie at the base of my soul. Much of the feeling and tone of this book is a result of that homework.

This story is very much a product of family, beginning with my mother's family who were farmers and ranchers. They lived close to the land and embodied in themselves a trust of animals, intuitions of the weather, and the feelings that come with different seasons of the year. I was raised on family stories such as the following: When my mother was in grade four she and her older sister rode a horse several miles to school. One winter day a snowstorm suddenly came up. When school was let out early, my mother and aunt got on the horse and headed home. The storm got worse. Soon they were in a constant whiteout. The wind howled so loudly that they could hardly hear each other speak. They were lost and thought they were going to freeze to death. They decided to trust the horse. So they dropped the reins and "gave the horse its head." The horse took them right to the barn. The family rejoiced. As people of the land they knew that every animal had senses unique to its particular nature, senses that were beyond the human and that could be trusted. Years later my mother developed a special devotion to Our Lady of the Snows. But I don't think "Mrs. Mare" ever knew the origin of her love for that wild spirit protectress. I found these sentiments well preserved within me as I peeled off layers of rational education.

I also found preserved in my early life the unconscious of my father's family. His mother suffered from mental illness. She was forcibly taken from the family home by the Royal Canadian Mounted Police during an acute exacerbation of her illness in 1921. She was committed to a provincial mental hospital under the Mental Diseases Act and never returned to the family. She died there in 1955. The mystery of her departure and the forgetting of her person by the family left an unconscious imprint that I found as I moved from being a Western psychiatrist to an Eastern philosopher and then back to restart my life as a natural person. The importance of the roots of my parental families cannot be told here but suffice it to say that in my relationship with another spirit guide I was able to make reconnections with important aspects of my family's soul, so that I can now celebrate the fears and joys that lay at the base of both family systems.

The flow of this story is presented in as rational a manner as I could organize the material. There were, in fact, some logical progressions over the years. What I could not do, either because of lack of skill or because readers would become confused by the introduction of what might be called the Indian way of teaching, is present the material in the surprising ways it came to me, because it would appear "disorganized." Nevertheless, the reader will come, I think, to appreciate the progression of the unfolding of some of the "secrets" coded into the effigy mounds and an introduction into aspects of the North American Indian philosophy of the medicine wheel. But should there ever be another opportunity, I might try to explain these lessons as they, in fact, came to me.

For Native Americans, however, no lesson was considered closed or finished. Lessons ended with an open gestalt, with mystery, and the student was expected to bring the lesson to his or her own "conclusion." The information shared with a "student" depended on the ability of the student to understand and use it. Since native peoples around the world were more biologically oriented, their "stories" took into account the three natural "ages" of "wo/man," that is, the child, the adult, and the aged. These three biological ages, pre-puberty, maturity, and post-menopausal, are in fact distinct cognitive and emotional phases of life, which lay the base for the roles and the potential dynamics of each phase. It is not therefore surprising that there are different levels of information "coded" into each mounds construction. It should also not come as surprise, then, that I have devoted a separate chapter to each age group. Bear with me when you come to these chapters, as I state and restate some of the information. Natives taught and learned by a process of increasing approximation, usually "taught" by imitative doing, so that once the student had digested a lesson, more information was shared, building on the past. Our culture teaches in a similar way but with the addition of books and the computer the student can always fast-forward by looking up the answers in the back of the book, so to speak. Our focus is more on getting right answers. We live in a very different world. But for the sake of this lesson for us, we must understand that Indians taught by repetition and by doing, which is a different process.

Nevertheless, I hope you will enter this journey and come to understand a first approximation to the world view of the Native American, a world view governed by natural processes that had the sun and the moon as cyclic guardians, that knew the ways of plants and animals, that knew the geometry of the forests, and the sets of relationships that we are only now coming to embrace in our concepts of interdependence and ecology. (As John Muir said, the trouble with studying anything is that it is hitched to everything else.) Moreover, they were cultures that planned for the seventh future generation. By comparison, I am in touch with three generations—my parents, mine, and my children's. But my grandparents' generation makes progressive sense these days, and I await my own grandchildren. So while my sense of generation grows in a "fast-food" world, it falls short of the wisdom of elder cultures. It is my opinion that the wisdom of the American Indian nations can now be shared with Euro-Americans in a fruitful and beneficial manner. The time has come to re-introduce the philosophy of the medicine wheel so that it may take its place among the great philosophies of the world. In order to facilitate this mission, let me introduce a voice that will speak here and there throughout the story. Italicized sentences will identify this voice as it gives authority to the message.

Since the beginning of conscious time, all peoples have intuited their innate connectedness with the spiritual aspect of reality, with the unseen world that underlies the physical world. As cultures evolved, they developed symbols and other means to help maintain contact between both worlds so they could remain in balance. The Greeks concluded that the whole Earth as they knew it was conscious and alive. They called her Gaia.² They saw Earth as a great conscious mother of which each person was a conscious living part. They believed in the transformation of each human being through the life cycle and they recognized that the apparent forces of good and evil needed a geography to play out their drama, and thus the gods were placed on the top of Mount Olympus and the demonic forces were placed in the underworld. Sometimes the Fates and the Muses communicated the wills of these archetypal realms to the mortals who played out their drama on the surface of the earth.

Other cultures around the world shared similar ideas and developed similar means to aid in their communication with the archetypal forces. The North American Indian nations felt that the earth as they knew it rested on the back of a giant turtle. They called North America "Turtle Island." Much as the Hindus believed that the earth was resting on four elephants who were standing on the back of a turtle, swimming through the ether, the Native Americans believed that they were living on the back of a turtle that was swimming through the ether. In their quest to return to the archetypal good, they called the Unseen the "Great Spirit," or for the Ho-Chunk, "Wakan Tanka," they believed that some animals were special envoys from the Great Spirit. These totem animals helped keep the tribe in balance with the natural world and the unseen spirit world. Thus, for the Indians of the plains who fed on the buffalo, the buffalo were sacred. The Indians of the Northwest, who fed on salmon, had salmon as their cultural totem. And so, too, the caribou and seal in the north, and the deer and other animals in the forests, took on a transcendent quality.

I share these thoughts before you go on the journey through the Mounds because I am a manifestation of the turtle spirit. My name is Nottwo. Over time, it has been my duty and pleasure to inform the spiritual consciousness of Native American heroes on their quest to help their people live in balance with nature. I was alive and vigorous until the whites came, starting historical time. The story that is about to unfold concerns the going and return of the Eagle Clan of the Ho-Chunk people.

The Ho-Chunk Nation lived in the place now called Wisconsin. Other peoples migrated through this land, but this was their home. They maintained their borders sometimes through warfare with their neighbors, and over the generations they developed a culture that had all the facets of completeness. Their oral tradition, their songs, their dances and way of life were sophisticated, but their art and writing in the form of effigy mounds could be said to be the best statement of their maturation as a people. When the whites came, the mounds were desecrated. More than 80 percent have been destroyed. Those that remain have grown "cold." Through-out this story, the sentiments and impressions of those people who have become friendly to the preservation and resurrection of the Mounds will have found inspiration through me. I am the spirit of the land and am dedicated to preserve the spiritual history of Native Americans.

Chapter I

EQUANIMITY
Living in harmony

Y our journey will begin in the North and rotate with the sun
to the East, the South, and the West. Wisdom from the North
and illumination from the rising sun will give birth to innocence in the South, in order to prepare you for death in the West.
*Your movement in the compass of space and time will bring you to
the still point in the immovable spot. The long body of your life will
illustrate the process of identification and point to the medicine that
can heal the illusion of separation.*

— Nottwo

*Of all the creatures of the universe it is we alone who do not
begin our lives with knowledge of this great harmony . . . to determine this place we must learn to give away . . . a vision quest or
perceiving quest is the way we must begin this search.*

— Hyemeyohsts Storm

The night was clear. The moon was full. The stars were bright.
Sparks from two fires sprayed up toward the heavens in wild and
timeless cascades, dancing with the stars. Around the fires the Ho-
Chunk had entrained their spirits to the sound of the drums. The
beat gave an auditory structure to the dance of the fire and the
sparkle of the stars.

Members of the Ho-Chunk Eagle and Turtle clans had gathered
on the south shore of the lake now called Lake Mendota, in Madison, Wisconsin, to celebrate their long history of living in the area
and to look for signs that would guide the Eagle Clan, since they

had made the decision to move west. Fires were warming rocks that would soon be placed in the two sweat lodges. Chiefs of both the Eagle and Turtle clans came to the middle point of the gathering between the two fires, and after ceremonial acknowledgment the chief of the Eagle Clan said, "Our clans used to live down on the Great Mississippi River. We came up the Wisconsin together to this area. We have lived here in harmony. These mounds, this Eagle and this Turtle, were made to celebrate the harmony that we shared living in this place. It is a joy to remember the great life we have had together here. It is with sadness that we say to you that it is time, brothers and sisters, for the Eagles to move west. We ask that you share the power of your sweat lodge with us as we look for signs to give strength and determination to our journey."

In turn, the chief of the Turtle Clan stepped forward and, with great ceremony, reaffirmed that the Eagle and Turtle mounds immediately behind them had been constructed as statements of the brother and sisterly love between the clans, and that they would, indeed, join in a sweat to seek signs that would help guide the Eagles on their journey. This said, each chief moved to the fire in front of his clan mound while the drumming continued.

Thirteen men from each clan were preparing for the sweat. They were members of the Sweat Lodge and were familiar with the ritual. They knew it would cleanse them and nourish them. Because word had come from Milwaukee that white soldiers and priests had made contact with the their Eastern brothers, they were concerned for their welfare. And while some of the Turtle, Bear, and Fox Clan were excited by the possibility of trade, members of the Eagle Clan interpreted the intrusion of these foreigners as a bad omen. They could not be trusted. Word from other tribes talked of trade, a search for the Salt Sea to the west, a growing demand for land, and, worst of all, settlements for the Whites. The six nations of the Iroquois were themselves confused about the invasion. These signs told the Eagles, with their high place of illumination, to move West. Here, then, on the south shore of the lake the Ho-Chunk called *Wonk Shek Ho-Mikla*, the Place Where The People Died and are Buried, the fires had now surrendered their heat to the rocks.[1]

Each sweat lodge was made of willow saplings. They were bound together with straps of bark. The willow skeleton shaped in the form of a turtle shell was about four feet high at the center. It was covered with deer hides. In the center of the lodge, a pit one and a half feet round and one foot deep, would hold the heated rocks. From this pit in the center of the lodge, a line was drawn due west through the door of the lodge to the fire pit that was transforming the rocks.[2]

The drums went silent, and one by one men of the Eagle Clan entered their lodge. Nude, each came to the door to the left of the line connecting the center pit and the fire. With a last look at the stars, each knelt and, on all fours, entered the lodge and, crawling to the left, moved clockwise around the rock pit. The first warrior stopped when he came to the spot near the door on the other side of the imaginary line. "All my relatives" was the ritual prayer he uttered as he entered, the lodge.

Before the last warrior entered, he used a forked stick to move each of twenty-eight hot rocks, one at a time, into the lodge.[3] The Sweat Celebrant directed the placement of the first seven rocks. The first rock was placed on the west side of the pit. Other rocks were then placed in clockwise order to the north, east, and south. Then a center rock was positioned in the middle, representing the interior life of each person, the place where Wakan Tanka dwells. A rock symbolizing the heavens was placed on the center rock. A seventh rock was placed beside the center rock, symbolizing the earth beneath. Thus, the seven sacred directions were honored, the four directions of the compass, and above, below and within.

The remaining twenty-one rocks were placed randomly in the pit. When they had found their resting places, the last Eagle entered the lodge. The flap was lowered, covering the door and sealing the lodge from the outside world. It was transformed into an earth womb. The warriors were now symbolically inside a turtle, symbolically because a sweat lodge was usually constructed to resemble a turtle; all clans had agreed on this design. The "mind" of the turtle, energized by heating the rocks in the fire pit outside the lodge, was now glowing in the pit in the middle of the lodge. The orange-red rocks representing the wisdom of the turtle, had been brought inside the lodge/turtle shell, as a turtle brings in its head, protecting it next to its heart. Hot wisdom glowed from the rock pit, enriching the beating hearts of the warriors. The glow of the rocks strengthened the hopeful attitude pulsating inside.

The Sweat Celebrant offered a few words to clarify their collective intention. Then, with a rush of excited energy, they broke into wild song. Air rushed from their lungs as they called on the spirit of each direction to join them. They honored each direction with full-throated enthusiasm. After they had toasted each direction, water was splashed on the rocks. The hiss and spit of the water brought bursts of steam that filled the lodge with intense heat. The chemistry of vigorous song and oppressive heat started a regressive process that they hoped would result in a vision. Already "tuned" by the drumming, the warriors now willfully poured themselves out in song, in sweat, in the communion of the sacred lodge.

The directions honored, more water was poured onto the rocks. Silence fell over the dark lodge. Then, in clockwise order starting with the last to enter the lodge, each man, in turn, prayed to Wakan Tanka, the Great Spirit, "Oh, Great Spirit, we honor You in Your creation. We honor the earth and the soil. We honor our cousins the plants and trees. We honor our two-legged and four-legged brothers. We honor our winged sisters. We honor all our relatives, the rocks and the rivers, the clouds and the stars. We honor you, grandmother and grandfather. We honor the Ho-Chunk, our ancestral roots. We honor the mothers and warriors that create and protect our nation. We honor the deer and the sacred corn that feed us. We honor the eagle, our sacred animal." Each of the men offered these prayers of praise, but each also spoke of their strengths and limits, their fears and hopes. They asked for help, confessed their transgressions, and vowed their amends. While the prayer round was at once an intimate profession of solidarity and a confession of the limits of their manhood, this sweat was unique because for the first time in many cycles of the moon, each of them petitioned the Great Spirit for guidance about the same thing. They had not met these White foreigners and they did not know what to make of their wonders. Iron knives were already replacing the bone. Fire sticks were frightening. The power of White medicine was strong.

They called on their ancestors to show them the way. When the last man had made his prayer, more water was poured on the rocks, causing the glow to fade. Since the lodge was hot, the door was opened to let some of the steam escape. Then, after a few minutes, the celebrant lit the pipe to start the third round. Each member of the lodge had a sacred ceremonial pipe.[4] In each sweat one or more pipes were loaded with sacred tobacco and placed just outside the lodge near the door. Because the first two rounds of the sweat produced significant steam, the tobacco would become too wet to light if it were kept inside the lodge, thus pipes were left outside the door. When the door was opened, the steam escaped, and the pipe—only one would be used for this sweat—was lit. Then the door was closed and again, one by one, starting with the last to enter the lodge, each took the pipe, offered it to the Great Spirit, inhaled two or three puffs of smoke, exhaled, offered the pipe bowl to the four directions, and then handed it in silence to the man on his left. The silence and the smoke weighed on each of the men. The sublimation of the smoke began an inspirational process in each man.

The tobacco was sacred. This was a special medicine, but there was nothing in it that, of itself, would cause visions.[5] The process of dehydration, meditation, and celebration were the ingredients that offered the spirit of each man the opportunity to look beyond his usual perception of the world. The magic of this earth womb, the sweat lodge, offered the celebrants an opportunity to open to the great mystery, and just as they had when they passed from childhood to adulthood in the vision quest, they waited for a sign, for a vision.

At first, the stones simply appeared to glow quietly. Water had caused a powerful rush of steam to bellow up and out, engulfing the warriors. But the rush of heat that followed acted as a collective shock, for as it passed they could all see in the black mist that continued to emerge from the pit a green-white form. From every point in the circle, each saw the same clear mist-laden spirit, greenish-white. It rolled over and over like a ball of smoke curling up to the sky.

The green-white mirage grew in clarity and began to crystallize into the form of a turtle. The turtle, about the size of a small gourd, stood still until every warrior had fixed the form in his visual mind with constant attention. The sudden rush of steam had first overwhelmed them, but as the mirage crystallized, capturing their attention, it held just long enough to organize the cognitive realm and then in a further transformation, their collective mind was held constant. They seemed to enter the image of the turtle, and as they did the image grew to fill the lodge. Then the turtle blew out of the lodge into the infinity of space, and in the blowout, the spirit of each warrior surrendered into the eternal mystery.

Beyond the bounds of their physical and mental forms, but aligned in spirit, the warriors heard the spirit of the Turtle say, *I am the earth. I am life. I am the heavens. I am the unity of these three. I am one, indivisible. I am neither this, nor that. I cannot be divided. I am one without a second. My name is Nottwo. In the past in this place, your grandmother and grandfather loved each other. They loved and honored the plants and their brothers, the two-legged and four-legged and the winged. Remember, then, your history as embodied in your brother ancestors, Walking Deer, Great Bear, and Two Dogs. And beyond the telling in words of the burial of these honored members of the Eagle Clan, remember that they lived as told to you by Nottwo, so you, the future ancestors of this sacred place, can know that the People have always honored each other and their brothers and sisters.*

Nottwo then said, Walking Deer, chief and shaman of the Eagle People, left the earth to start his journey to the Great Spirit. Old age had overtaken the sage, and his people were ready to prepare his place of rest. Walking Deer had lived more than seventy winters. He was a soul-mate of the medicine woman Great Bear. For sixty winters they had shared the wonders of the surrounding world. In good times and bad they had kept the spirit of the Eagle Clan tuned to the cycles. When Great Bear was told of the death of Walking Deer, she turned, closed her eyes, and gave her spirit back to Wakan Tanka.

Their bodies were taken to the prominent point at the headwaters of these lakes. A traditional tomb was constructed. The topsoil was removed. A base of rocks was laid. The bodies, dressed in ceremonial clothes, were brought to the site. Then tragedy struck. Two Dogs, a boy of six winters, was killed in an accident. The boy, already enchanted and picked for the Lodge, was close to both sages. His body was prepared and he was brought to the site. Walking Deer and Two Dogs were placed on the bottom rocks of the tomb. Walking Deer was placed on the west side with Two Dogs behind him. Both were placed in a seated position, facing the setting sun.[6] The stone walls of the tomb were built up around them. Their bodies were packed in dirt. When they were covered, an oval cluster of stones was placed in the middle of the grave. Then Great Bear was buried directly above Walking Deer, seated facing west. The stone mortuary was then closed. Sacred soil and special grasses were then planted. I tell you, remember your Clan ancestors lived here.

The intensity of the experience overwhelmed the warriors. Their spirits witnessed not just the great, infinite form and image of the turtle, but because their hearts and minds were aligned they could embrace these sacred words. When Nottwo had finished, they intuited the questions that lay before them, where should they go and when should they leave?

Nottwo, sensitive to their questions, told them that the Eagles should wait one winter and then take the Wisconsin River down to the Great River. They should follow its course until they reached a place that would later be known as Oklahoma. He said the time for travel would be when day and night were in balance in the following spring. He then told them that much change would occur before the forgotten spirit of their Eagle Clan would be remembered and return, and that that would occur at the time of the return of the white buffalo calf woman.

As quickly as they had exploded into transcendent space, the scene imploded, reversing itself, and they traveled back to the lodge. They were exuberant, joyful, ecstatic. United, they broke into the final round of song, completing the sweat. The sweat lasted several hours. Those outside the lodge could hear the magnificent chorus of singing, and it told them that the goal of the sweat had surely have been accomplished. Just before daybreak, the warriors of the Eagle Clan emerged from the sweat. They were spent. Their total surrender had drained them of themselves, but though tired, they emerged as victors of a strange struggle, possessing infinite energy that they would communicate to all members of their clan.

As the Eagles had been preparing for the sweat, so too had the Turtles. They, in like manner, had gone through the four rounds and they emerged from their sweat lodge equally wondrous. They too had entered a vision of the turtle Nottwo. They too were given the message that the Eagles should leave on their journey, west, down the Wisconsin on the day in the spring when the world is in balance.

As the thirteen members of each of the Clans emerged from the lodges and had taken positions around the central fire, the chiefs approached to close the ceremony. First they pointed to the south, where other members of both clans were celebrating at Spirit Rock. They then pointed to the west, where they celebrated the land of darkness and death. Then, looking north across the lake, they could see the fires of members of the Eagle and Fox Clans enacting the same ritual as the Eagle and Turtle Clans, asking guidance and support from their brother Clans. And they could see across the lake on the high point of the ground the burial place of Walking Deer, Great Bear and Two Dogs.

Finally, they looked to the east. As they did so, the light of the sun was just starting to appear, about to extinguish the stars. But out of the pattern of the still shining stars, to the north of east, they saw the image of the great medicine symbol of the north, the white buffalo, emerge and become clearer and clearer in the sky. Its wild, white hair started to shimmer and move. Members of both Clans were struck by this heavenly sign. The white buffalo, an image now distinct from the stars, magnificent in size, walked from its position in the north, perceptibly and obviously, to the west and disappeared as the sunlight of the new day increased. The Eagles knew then that the wisdom of the north, the same wisdom imparted to them from the mind and heart of the Turtle in the sweats, would guide them on their migratory journey. Much would pass before the signs would be right for their return. The return of White Buffalo Calf Woman would pass before members of the Eagle Clan would walk over this sacred place again.

Whites, don't be confused. Native Americans related to a broad spectrum of totem animals in their spiritual conversations. Thus, there is nothing unusual for the Eagle Clan to find in their vision, the effigy spirit of another clan. Since their decision to move west was perhaps not one of illumination, it was appropriate that the most Earth-bound spirit take on the responsibility of guiding these sweats. Naturally, my appearance in the sweat lodge of the Turtle Clan was no surprise, but neither were the Eagles surprised by my appearance. Native Americans knew that the whole world was alive and that each living form had its spiritual aspect. If you are a Christian who hoped for a vision of Christ but instead had a vision of your patron saint, you are getting the idea. Try to become comfortable with this dimension as you open yourself to other experiences of the spirit.

Chapter II

EXCAVATION
Disturbing the Dead

A rock pile ceases to be a rock pile the moment a single man contemplates it, bearing within him the image of a cathedral.

— Antoine de Saint-Exupery

A man has made at least a start on discovering the meaning of human life when he plants shade trees under which he knows full well he will never sit.

— D. Elton Trueblood

The first rays of the sun were just beginning to awaken the still lake. It was, by one system of reckoning time, 1876. Dr. DeHarte, the superintendent of the State Hospital for the Insane in Madison, Wisconsin, and some of his colleagues left the main hospital building and walked down the sidewalk, south towards Lake Mendota. They were quite excited. They had reached a point in the excavation of the largest conical mound in which they had penetrated two outer layers of the stone casing of the tomb, digging through the earth and contacting what appeared to be a body. The mound was a grave, and it was about to yield its dead.

From the beginning of the process of the excavation, now entering the third day, they had been in the habit of starting each day by walking down to the lake past the three large eagle effigy mounds. This morning was no different. At 6:30, the sun had broken the horizon. As they proceeded down the sidewalk, Dr. DeHarte motioned to his colleagues to look over to the left, where they saw the rise of the wing of the second largest eagle effigy mound on the hospital grounds. This bird was flying in a southeasterly direction. The ridge of the wing rose up approximately four feet above the landscape. About twenty yards in front of the eagle, a large bear mound had been placed on the flat landscape between the eagle and the lake.

They left the sidewalk when they reached the wing of the largest effigy eagle, which lay on their right. They were in the habit of walking in front of the wing towards the head and body of the eagle. The eagle was magnificent, even awe-inspiring. They had determined that the total wingspan was over six hundred feet. The body was over 130 feet in length. They were entranced as the sun came up, casting a shadow on the northwest side of the wing of the bird. They walked in silence, pondering nature's sounds, wondering whether these beautiful effigies were connected with the burial mound that they were excavating.

Pausing respectfully, they stood at the place where the head of the eagle rested. Even though the summer grass had grown high, it was clear that the beak of the eagle was pointing to the right wing. They stood before the massive bird looking to the head and body rising six feet above the surrounding land. They then walked on, now in front of the right wing of the great bird, and shortly they were also walking behind the left wing of the smallest eagle that was flying in front of the great eagle, but parallel with it. The smaller eagle was about half the size of the larger. These two eagles were clearly flying "in formation." Their line of flight would have caused them to intersect with the second largest eagle, first noted on the far left, just across the lake before a sharp rise in the land, called Maple Bluff, important now because it is the site of the Governor's mansion. After noting this curiosity they walked behind the tail of the smaller eagle and then on to what was called the old Indian trail.

The Indian trail was a well worn path that ringed Lake Mendota. At points it went within five feet of the lake and at others it went inland about twenty feet. It followed the natural contour of the land. They took it as they walked until after about ten minutes it brought them to the high point of the grounds. There, it was alleged that ancestors of the Ho-Chunk, sometimes called the Mound Builders, had sculpted seven conical mounds and a turtle effigy mound. A little to the east were several linear mounds, a large conical mound, and several other effigy mounds. Dr. DeHarte had started his excavation with the largest conical mound, on the highest point of the land.

As they walked towards this conical mound, Dr. DeHarte explained to his colleagues that a Ho-Chunk Elder, John Two Bears, had told him that the effigy mounds told stories, much like chapters in our books. Dr. DeHarte had asked John Two Bears many times to explain what this meant, but he would go no further. He asked John, of the Bear Clan, if he knew the stories, but John was not forthcoming. He said simply that the ancient ones had constructed these mounds and that each cluster told a specific story, but he stopped short of describing what the mounds on the grounds of the hospital might mean, or even whether he knew the stories. Of greater interest however, was a statement that another of the Ho-Chunk elders had made to Dr. DeHarte, and that was that the mounds were alive. Dr. DeHarte was puzzled by this statement. He did not know in what way the mounds could be alive. Were they alive symbolically? He wondered whether the elder had meant that the mounds were alive in the spirit world. He pondered this for several years and on a chance meeting with the elder about three years after the elder had made that statement he asked with some humility if the elder would explain how the mounds were alive. The elder could see that Dr. DeHarte was earnestly searching for an understanding of the sense of aliveness and he said, cryptically, "Let the mounds animals move in the direction that they would if they were alive and you will discover their message." But this did not help quiet Dr. DeHarte's questions.

It was perhaps seven o'clock in the morning when the group reached the excavation site. They had been working for two days digging down into the principal mound. (See Figure 2.) It was approximately fifteen feet high, thirty feet across, and a hundred feet long. They had decided to approach the excavation from the south side and had therefore dug two lines, one vertical and the other horizontal, until they arrived at a stone structure that was approximately four feet inside the earth. They cleared away a significant amount of earth until they could see a well defined stone chamber. The chamber was cleared on about a third of its southern side from the top of the mound to ground level. They were faced with a uniform "masoned" stone structure. The day before they had decided to break into it. They picked a spot, chipped away the stone, and discovered that the wall of the tomb actually consisted of a double row of stones. Inside the stone barrier there was packed earth. They had no idea what to expect as they dug into the earth of the mound, but they persevered until they came to what was clearly a skeleton, apparently buried in a seated position. That day they uncovered approximately half of the skeleton, from the skull down to the pelvis. They had the skull bone, the vertebrae, the ribs, the arms, and much of the lower

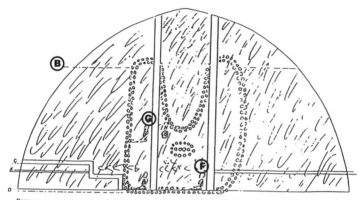

DESCRIPTION AND ORDER OF THE BURIALS.—A. Perpendicular shaft, B and E. Groups of stones found by the excavators 5 feet, below summit; next a layer of yellow clay about 4 feet deep. C, a drift made into the side 3 feet above the ground K.   D, bottom of the mound consisting of a bed of yellow clay. G, skeleton with perforated humerus, pieces of pottery and a stone implement. H, stones, ashes, charcoal and decayed wood. F, two skeletons, one of a child six year-old, the other of an adult; found with pieces of pottery and two stone implements, 1½ feet below the surface of the ground.

Figure 2. The burial mound on the grounds of the Mendota Mental Health Institute, in Madison, Wisconsin, excavated by Dr. DeHarte in 1876. The stone chamber marked "B" contained three skeletons, two adults under "G" and a child at "F."

spine. There was no evidence that it was clothed. It appeared to be facing west. They planned to remove the rest of the skeleton that day, drawing and documenting as they went.

For shame, such desecration. Why, why need these Whites disturb my ancestors. Would they dig up their own grandparents? Have they no sense of their ancestors? Do they not understand that all people need and deserve respect?

The two labored until they could identify the bones of a complete adult skeleton. These were laid out on the ground. While they could not tell if it was a male or female, it was clearly an adult, the bones indicating a person approximately 5'6." There were no obvious fractures or obvious evidence of disease. They were quite impressed and excited and they resolved to continue the excavation.

It would take two more days for them to complete the excavation of the inside of the grave. In the process they would discover a second adult skeleton placed in a seated position immediately below the first adult, and they would find the skeleton of a child approximately six to eight years old buried, also in a sitting position, on the same plane as the adult in the lower part of the tomb, and behind. Thus, two adults and a child were buried in the stone chamber. Dr. DeHarte later wrote that he had sent the skeletons to the Smithsonian Institution in Washington, D.C.

On this particular day, however, the excavation proceeded on the one side until they had uncovered the second adult. The investigators were ecstatic over their find. There was little precedent for excavating the mounds[1]. While some "archaeologists" in other states had excavated mounds, there was no system of approval or review, no standards, no informed consultants to help guide these "pioneers." In spite of this, Dr. DeHarte had formulated a plan. First he determined the height of each mound and the circumference at the base. Then he identified the height of each mound in the cluster, using the water level of the lake as the base. For instance, he estimated that the largest conical mound, the one they were in the process of excavating, was 96 feet above lake level. In a similar manner he measured the height of all of the other mounds, which ranged from 86 to 96 feet above lake level. The turtle was the closest to the water line. At its highest point it was approximately 90 feet above the lake level, but at its lowest point it was approximately 86 feet. The turtle appeared to be going down the hill, an observation that did not escape Dr. DeHarte's eye. He simply had no idea what it could mean.

They broke early in the afternoon, when the sun had crested in the sky. It was hot. The group decided to climb onto the back of the turtle mound, the only effigy placed in proximity to the seven conical mounds. Sitting on the back of the turtle, Dr. DeHarte noticed that the turtle had a long axis to its body and that when one sat on its back, looking toward the turtle's head and the lake, the sight line seemed to continue to a distant hillock across the lake, on the relatively flat horizon to the northwest.

While Dr. DeHarte and his colleagues sat on the turtle mound, they discussed, as others had, the meaning of the mounds. He knew the theory that they had been constructed by ancient Indian people. He knew there was another theory that the builders were a special people called the Mounds Builders and that they were now extinct.[2] He was more immediately aware that the Ho-Chunk, indigenous natives to this part of the world from the origins of time, said that the mounds were built by their ancestors. He also knew that some people in Washington held rather wild views that the effigy mounds were built by the lost tribes of Israel. And thus it was that after the Civil War, Dr. DeHarte and others like him began examining the mounds, attempting to discover their meaning and origins. For his part he felt privileged to be able to dig into an ancient grave and with all the respect that he could mount, describe its contents with the hope that a greater understanding of the mounds would result. He hoped they would be protected from desecration and destruction. Farmers were already plowing them flat. He did not feel that he was intruding into the grave of recently buried people. That was simply because the local Ho-Chunk talked about these as burials of ancient ancestors and without any reference to an intimate knowledge of the actual people buried there. He had, before he entered into the decision to excavate, consulted local religious leaders and had made an attempt to talk with elders of the Ho-Chunk to raise this very issue. Unfortunately, he was not able to communicate directly with any knowledgeable authoritative Ho-Chunk, including his friend John Two Bears, and as a result the Ho-Chunk had not been properly consulted. The Christian ministers and priest with whom he did consult raised no objections to "the advance of science" and encouraged him in his pursuit of knowledge.

This was not the only limitation. Dr. DeHarte was aware that the Ho-Chunk Nation was divided into clans, like the Scots. He knew that each clan was identified with a totem animal. In fact, the Ho-Chunk elder, John Two Bears, with whom he talked from time to time, was a member of the Bear Clan. He was told that the Fox, Deer, Buffalo, Hawk, and Turtle Clans were well represented in Wisconsin. Of course he knew the Ho-Chunk had been removed from Wisconsin following the "treaties" after the Blackhawk War of 1832.[3] Many, it was said, were "resettled" in northern Nebraska, but most had returned to their ancestral lands in Wisconsin. It was a curiosity that he could not find a member of the Eagle Clan. They were simply gone. John Two Bears was silent about their absence. Since the eagle mounds that drew his interest were so prevalent, he longed to ask a member of the Eagle Clan what the eagle effigy mounds meant, and ask them whether they knew the names or clan of the people buried in the graves.

By the end of the day, Dr. DeHarte and his colleagues had completed the excavation of half of the contents of the stone chamber. They had discovered two magnificent, well preserved adult skeletons, each about the same height. They had worked under the bounty of a glorious sun. It was benevolently warm. They had, at times, been able to enjoy the scenic view from that high point of ground, surrounded on two sides by the water of Lake Mendota. In fact, if one looked to the northwest, one could see the water coming from the Yahara River, formerly known as the Catfish River, as it came out of Westport moving into the lake and then on across the Madison isthmus to Lake Monona, and from there down the four lake system to the Rock River and on to the Mississippi. This land, as it jut out into Lake Mendota's water, was as magnificent as the bluffs at Maple Bluff. Dr. DeHarte felt that the people who were buried on this high point must have indeed been prominent.

The group had gone back to the main hospital for dinner and then, retracing their steps, they returned to the area of excavation as the sun was going down. Sitting on the back of the turtle, Dr. DeHarte looked to the east and remembered the long progression of mounds that were associated with this group. Approximately a mile away due east, as he could figure, there was another prominent conical mound. Close to it were three fox-like mounds. Proceeding west from the fox mounds towards the conical that he was excavating were three thunderbird mounds. This then led to the three eagles that were located on the low plane of land below the main building of the hospital. In fact, he had been able to discuss these mounds with Reverend Peet, a Protestant minister, who had diagrammed the mounds, about fifty in all. Reverend Peet had divided them into three groups: the western group that Dr. DeHarte was working on, the central group, centering on the three large eagle effigies, and an eastern group, the thunderbirds, foxes, and conicals. Reverend Peet would publish his work in 1890.[4] He was fascinated by the mounds but could not enlighten Dr. DeHarte on the stories they told. So Dr. DeHarte and his colleagues were left to wonder why mounds like the eagles, the panther, the bear, and the deer, were placed where they were and what stories might they tell.

Chapter III

GREAT EXPECTATIONS
Surrending Spirits

I*f spirit is completely transcendent, it is also completely imminent. I am firmly convinced that if a new and comprehensive
paradigm is ever to emerge, that paradox will be its heart.*

— Ken Wilber

*Self-interest is but the survival of the animal in us. Humanity
only begins for man with self-surrender.*

— Henri Amiel

The warm air and clear sky made it easy to say goodbye to the
setting sun. Time, by the Christian system of reckoning, had moved
to the year 1979. I was sitting on the back of the turtle mound near
sunset at the beginning of June. The burial mound excavated by Dr.
DeHarte in 1876 and reported in 1877 was about thirty feet behind
me. I was aware that Dr. DeHarte had found three skeletons in a
stone tomb, and as a recovering Christian I had vaguely wondered
why the Indians had placed a turtle and not a dove, or at least some
kind of bird, as the spirit animal to lead the native souls to heaven.

I had moved from my home in Midland, Ontario, to Madison
in September, 1978. I was a forensic psychiatrist, the first director
of the Forensic Program at the Mendota Mental Health Institute,
formerly called the Mendota State Hospital, and, before that, the
State Hospital for the Insane. The former names had become stig-
matized because the term "state hospital" conjured up in the mind
of the public a poorly staffed madhouse for the hopelessly crazy.
The new name, Mental Health Institute, was the treatment for the

old, but reformation of the mental health system is another story. Suffice it to say that my long-standing interest in understanding the motivation of sexual and aggressive impulses as they related to mental illness and crime, and the role of the insanity defense, had drawn me to the job.

My other lifelong interest was understanding and adapting Native American philosophy to contemporary life. One of my uncles had been an Indian agent on a Blackfoot reservation in southern Alberta. As a child I had spent several summers playing with Indian kids on the reservation. Not only did I come to appreciate the natural freedom they enjoyed, I also heard their stories. In 1903 members of the Blackfoot Nation approached the fathers of the little mining town of Frank, which lay before the entrance to the Crowsnest Pass in southern Alberta and told them that the animals had moved off Turtle Mountain. They interpreted this sign to mean that the mountain, which lay south of the town across the valley, was unstable and was going to fall into the valley. According to the legend that grew after the slide, they said that the town of Frank was in danger and they urged the whites to move. The whites did not heed the warning and on April 29, 1903, the north face of Turtle Mountain crashed down into the valley, burying the town of Frank. At least seventy people were killed. The highway sign that once described the slide began with the Indian warning. But the staff at the Frank Slide Interpretive Center now say that the Indian warning is only part of the mythology of the slide and that it can not be historically documented.[1] But my uncle knew the "myth" was fact because the Indians had told him that they had warned the town.

Later in my psychiatric residency I was part of a small group of "Southern Canadians" who lived with the Dogrib and Slavey Indians, "Northern Canadians," part of one summer near Yellowknife in the Northwest Territories. There, our group of Southern Canadians adapted to the culture and earned enough trust to be invited to learn a chant and play at a drum dance[2]. I had also read about Native American cultures, by both white and Native American writers. I was convinced that Euro-Americans would one day want to learn how to live in harmony with this landmass and that the people who had lived here for millennia would perhaps at that time share their wisdom on how they did it.

Newly arrived in Wisconsin in 1978, my wife and I decided to take an apartment on the grounds of the Mendota Mental Health Institute until we could buy a house. The apartment was located right beside the conical mounds and the turtle mound. In fact, I went by these mounds every day on my way to and from work. During the spring of 1979 I noted that people seemed to enjoy the sunset while sitting on the back of the turtle. One evening in early June I was sitting there, cross-legged, enjoying the sunset, when I noticed that the sun was going to set about twenty degrees to the southwest of the spot on the horizon that the turtle pointed to. With some excitement, the idea occurred to me that perhaps the turtle had a meaningful alignment with the sun. Since the summer solstice was about three weeks away, I thought that perhaps the turtle was purposefully placed to point to the spot on the horizon where the sun would set on the longest day of the year, the summer solstice. Three weeks later on the summer solstice the sun had moved nearer to the spot which the turtle pointed to, but it fell short by seven or eight degrees, as best as I could measure with my hand compass. My excitement quieted and for awhile I lost interest in understanding the mounds.

On my journey to understand the mounds I had discovered a map drawn by Reverend Peet in 1870, of about fifty mounds on the north shore of Lake Mendota.[3] (See Figure 3.) This map was completed just after the hospital opened in 1860. The map showed what we came to define as three groups of mounds. The eastern group consisted of conical and linear mounds with fox and thunderbird effigies. The central group consisted of three large eagles with a deer, bear, panther, and other nondescript mounds. The western group consisted of the seven conical mounds and the effigy turtle, and a number of other linear and conical mounds. These mounds were drawn with all the skill the artist could muster, using only a land-based perspective.

I had also secured a diagram published by Dr. DeHarte in which he described the stone tomb and the positions of the three buried people. He also marked the lines that he used in excavating the mound. What was so fascinating about his drawing was the clear outline of skeletons in seated positions and how the two adults were aligned, seated one above the other, with a child seated on the same

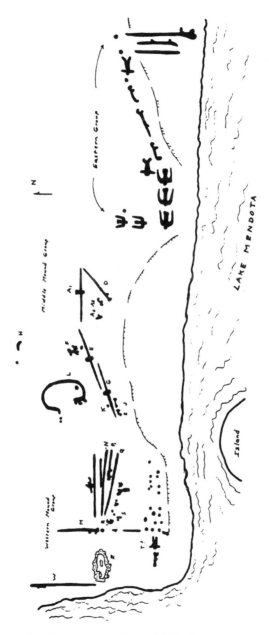

Figure 3. Examine these mounds again. Dr. DeHarte was able to examine them firsthand because they were still intact. The Eastern Group were progressively destroyed in the early 1900s.

plane behind the lower adult. The largest conical mound immediately behind the turtle was in fact the burial mound described by Dr. DeHarte, yet I continued to struggle with the placement of a turtle as the sole effigy associated with the conical group.

Time passed. One night in 1982 when I was on annual training with the Army Reserve at Fort Sam in San Antonio, I had a dream. As a child my oldest boy, Michael, had been allergic to the fur of cats and dogs, and as a result he had played with turtles, snakes, and other reptiles. Quite suddenly as I slept he appeared to me in a dream and said, "Dad, let me explain why the Indians used a turtle to guide the souls on their afterdeath journey." Delighted, I asked him to teach me, and in the lucid dream that followed he said, "They placed a turtle as the spirit guide for a number of reasons. First, a turtle looks like a conical mound. There is a similarity of form. Second, when a turtle pulls in its legs and head, it appears inert, it appears dead. But we know that the turtle is alive inside its shell. So, too, the three people buried in the stone grave appear to be dead but they are really still alive in the afterdeath realm. Third, if you look carefully at the turtle, you will notice that it is going down the hill. If it were given a push, it would go down to its natural habitat, the lake. Remember that turtles can live on land and in the water. They lay their eggs in the ground so the young are born to the surface of the earth. Because they can live for periods of time under water, the turtle is an excellent symbol of an animal that is aware of the surface world and the unseen world in the 'depths.' They are aware of the world above the surface of the land or water, and of the realms below the surface of the land or water. Dad, you are a psychiatrist, can you see that the turtle is aware of what is in the conscious world, what is above the surface, and what is in the unconscious world, what is below the surface in the 'underworld'? Can you see that this turtle represents an animal that can lead these souls on the journey down the hill, down below the surface of the lake, and ultimately down below the horizon of the earth?

"You wanted the turtle to point to the spot on the horizon where the summer solstice sun would set. And when it did not, you became frustrated. The reason they pointed the turtle to this spot was to show that in spite of the fact that the sun had set and it was now dark on the surface of the earth, the turtle, in its projected journey, would lead the souls to the place where the sun was still shining below the horizon. In other words, the turtle knows that the sun lives on after its apparent death to us on the land. The turtle knows of the sun's journey to the underworld before it rises again in the east. The turtle then is an animal envoy from the great unseen that unites light and dark, life and death. Because it can transition back and forth between both realms, it yokes life to death and death to life. It knows how one is part of the other and the relationship between the two."

Overjoyed with my son's insights, I "woke up" and after sharing the dream with my wife, I wrote it down.[4] It came as an inspiration, as an encouragement to me that the effort I had made to understand the meaning of the mounds was being rewarded. During the early years of my research I was motivated in part, but a significant part, by a desire for fame and fortune. I felt as though I would discover some fabulous tomb, full of golden artifacts and that like the opening of the tomb of Tutankhamen, vast riches would be uncovered and I, yes, me, I would be heralded for my cleverness. Good fortune, money, and TV appearances would follow. The stuff that our culture gives as a reward for creative discovery would be mine, even if it were just for fifteen minutes.

As the years passed I slowly identified and worked through greed. I identified that part of me that was just another capitalistic profiteer who would take from the Native Americans whatever I could without caring for their culture. Whereas others had killed the buffalo solely for its hide, or had dug the gold from the Black Hills without care for the sacredness of the Lakota land, my rip-off would come from exposing the untold hidden treasurers that lay in the mounds. In those days if you had asked me whether we should excavate the other conical mounds in the western group, I would have organized the party. Something in me wanted to be enriched by this history, but until I identified my ego greed lust, I would not be able to accept the personal and then spiritual lessons that awaited me. So I began to let go of the possessive and ego-driven aspects of my family and cultural imprinting. As I entered new realms of my personal faith journey it progressively became associated with the "natural person" in me. Like John Dunbar in *Dances With Wolves*, I began to move to the frontier of my personness. I began to encounter the "original" me, or the "natural" me. And when the vanguard of Western culture began to intrude as the army did in *Dances*, I moved on into my nature. I began to surrender to personal aspects of the journey, such as the connections with my children and relearning how to be a child. I slowly became a servant of the mounds, dedicating more and more of my time to the basic research needed to discover the role the mounds played in describing Native American life. My son, Michael, had entered my dream life at a time when I was able to respond.

After the dream it occurred to me that this may not be a chance event. Further, I wondered whether in fact there was anything that I could do to actively encourage the process of understanding the mounds beyond literature searches. By becoming more aware of the dream realm, recognizing my cultural set may not allow "forbidden" aspects of the mounds to enter the cognitive realm of day. As I looked within myself for other models that might help me, I realized that I had been in a relationship with the turtle mound for some time and that in fact the turtle, if it was personified and given respect, might become a living symbol that could help transform not just my knowledge of the mounds but transform me in a larger way. Thus it was that night I decided to actively communicate with the turtle as though it was alive. I would talk with it, ask it questions, and share my concerns. The relationship that I had had with my guardian angel as a young Catholic, though unpracticed for years, came alive with Nottwo the turtle. I asked the turtle to become my guardian spirit, and I had the clear impression that that is what happened.

It was at this point that I also began a journal which over the years became filled with impressions, observations, thoughts, reveries, intuitions, and other associations that I came to understand as gifts from Nottwo, the name of the turtle spirit of the turtle mound. As my private relationship with Nottwo took on greater and greater reality, unknowing family and friends began to "unconsciously" send me pictures of turtles and turtle statues. I found that as my relationship grew with Nottwo, my insights into the cognitive and intuitive realms of the mounds and of myself also grew. Nottwo did not speak to me in English, and while Nottwo did appear at times in dreams, these were rare occurrences.[5] I came to know that Nottwo was communicating with me by the associations surrounding an insight into the mounds, by the timing of a "chance" literature reference or, more powerfully, usually at night when I would "see" another way native people saw the world they lived in and could make an adaptation in my life from that point on to see that point of view for myself.

These insights focused mainly on the associative syntax of the grouping of particular mounds, but over time my thinking, or thought patterns, began to transform from a Judeo-Christian paradigm of dominion, to a native paradigm of relationship. At the hospital this process of change was identified by peers as moving from a power-oriented paradigm to a "respect for all staff" paradigm. In this later paradigm all living beings are co-equal, equally respected, but with different strengths and lessons to teach. The so-called lower animal level of existence was not to be dominated by the so-called higher, but rather lived with. By 1988 I could identify with Rianne Eisler, my thinking had moved from a "dominator model" to a "partnership model."[6] This change in conceptual orientation was in part a gift from Nottwo, and the "mounds."

Let me share the kind of experience that I had again and again, as I moved from my Western-shaped conception of the world to what I found well developed in me and identified as a native or natural person's conception of the world. As a child I had lived by rivers. By the time I was five we had moved to Edmonton, Alberta, on the banks of the North Saskatchewan River. We lived on Jasper Avenue near 92nd Street in an apartment complex. The hill leading down to the river was immediately across the road. The river was in a valley perhaps two hundred feet below. I used to play with my friends "down the hill." This was an enchanted world of forest and wildlife. Choke cherries, raspberries, and strawberries were very abundant at different times of the year down the hill, and over several summers when I was five, six, and seven, it seemed natural for me to talk to the berry plants. As I plucked the berries I would thank the bushes for their fruit. "Thank you for the berries, they are really tasty. I love them. I am going to eat what I can now and I am going to take some in my pocket for later. But I want you to know that because you have satisfied my hunger, I am going to scatter your seeds all over this hill."

I actively communicated with the berry plants and felt a sense of kinship with them. Their fruit sustained me and somehow as a child I wanted to sustain them in return. As a consequence I consciously scattered their seeds all over the hill. By the time I had done this for three summers, I thought I could identify bushes that had grown from seeds that I had scattered.

Because I was a Catholic I went to a "separate school." We had a religion lesson every day. Part of the structure of the Baltimore catechism-driven classes included the use of a series of large charts. As I write this I can still remember the day when Miss Redman told us that Jesus was the Son of God. This was a hard idea for me to understand because the whole world was alive and "God" to me. I remember the difficulty I had trying to identify him with the place in me called God. Then one day Miss Redman started the lesson by flipping the chart to a picture of Jesus stilling the sea, with the Apostles frightened in the boat. Jesus had power over nature? I couldn't believe it but they said it was true and my teachers knew. It was at that exact moment that a veil, just like the chart, came down over my mind and I made the connection that she was telling me that the place that I had God in my life, which was best exemplified by the relationship I had with the berry bushes, was now going to be called Jesus Christ.

That experience was powerful. After that, my relationship with nature changed. I remember thinking summers later, as I ate berries from the bushes, that it was comforting to know that the person of Jesus Christ was looking over both of us, the plants and me. Many years later as I was returning to my "native self" I recovered this memory and this part of myself. The identification of this particular change in my perception of the world helped me understand why I have never lost my faith and trust in nature, why I never felt that nature was an "other" to be subjugated. I realized that the Christian myth had been laid on top of my natural relationship with the world. Perhaps even more important, however, was that this invigorated my identification with native peoples. I began to make the association more consciously between the relationship that I had had with berry plants that had nourished me and that I had wanted to nourish back by planting their seeds, and perhaps a more mature sense of my relationship with Christ. I made the analogy that the spiritual energy that had motivated me to treat a berry plant as sacred and as something that should be replenished could be considered the same spiritual energy that I had received from eating the body and blood of Christ in the form of communion at Mass. The Eucharist would nourish my body and soul, in turn I would then share "the good news" with others. I had been a partner with a plant in a relationship of mutual generation in the same way that during my days devoted to Catholicism I had become a soldier (a partner?) of Christ, receiving grace from the sacraments and in turn spreading the gospel.

Associations like these helped me to integrate the pre-Christian me with the Christian me. More important, I moved beyond a sole identification with the Christian myth. Because of the parallel dynamics embraced by all religions between the belief and the believer, or between the sacred food and the recipient, I could see how each "promoted" the other. Berries, or corn, buffalo, salmon, or caribou, natural people recognized the interdependence between themselves and the sacred food that sustained them. They recognized, in myth, legend, and story, the responsibility they had in turn to sustain their sacred food. Killing or harvesting then became a sacred act. For a Christian, Christ, as the last "bloody" sacrifice, is in reality another sacred food. But in prioritizing his message above all others, other religions and, sadly, nature became profane, to be dominated and subdued, as it says in Genesis.

Now as my relationship with Nottwo developed, and the "long body" of my life, that is the collection of my personal unconscious memories, began a new process of integration, I also discovered a community of people involved in a similar personal process, who were also interested in identifying, studying, and preserving the mounds. Soon I became part of a group that had founded a non-profit corporation called the Ancient Earthworks Society.[7] Some members of that group helped in 1986 to get the mounds protected under the Wisconsin Burial Sites Act. Later I sat on a subcommittee of the Dane County Parks Commission. The mounds were given further respect and protected from developers by giving each mound an area of 5 to 25 feet as a buffer between the outline of the mound and any new construction. At the same time, Jim Scherz, a professor of civil engineering at the University of Wisconsin-Madison, helped me to understand the sacred geometric relationships that he had found in his aerial surveys of many mound sites in Wisconsin.

All of these combined to help me expand my conception of Native Americans and the mounds, and also to understand the role that cyclic time played in their determinations, and to gain a greater understanding of the sacredness of place as it related to cyclic time. Furthermore, I was able to gain a growing understanding of the role of the effigy totem animal and make some approximation of the meaning of that animal to my Christian roots, finally identifying Christ as a sacred totem. But we'll leave that to later.

Following this first dream, much of my development and personal transformation occurred in the quiet of night, in coming to listen to the world and in developing an attitude of openness to the mystery of life. But it was in the broad light of day that I most shared my growing understanding of the mounds, of the life of symbolism of Native Americans and the interconnectedness of their lives with the living earth, plants, and animals. In 1982 I began to understand the mounds as the earth writing of the high culture of many of the nations of people native to the Americas. So one morning in 1985 I called Professor Scherz and asked him to conduct an aerial survey of the mounds on the grounds of Mendota Mental Health Institute.

Chapter IV

THE ENGINEER
The Eagle's View

I*f you can just observe what you are and move with it, then you will find that it is possible to go infinitely far.*

— J. Krishnamurti

Be patient toward all that is unsolved in your heart. And try to love the questions themselves.

—Rainer Maria Rilke

It was about ten o'clock in the morning one day in the summer of 1985. The sun was nearly overhead. The sky was cloudless. Professor Scherz and two students had just taken off from Truax Airport in Madison. They were in the process of conducting an aerial survey of the mounds on the grounds of the Mendota Mental Health Institute. They had flown over the grounds a number of times and had decided on the following course of action: They would level the plane off at about a thousand feet and using two cameras, stereo-scopically aligned, they would take a series of photographs of the grounds of the Institute and adjoining neighborhoods, which would give them clear images of the terrain. In this process, the students would learn how modern aerial survey techniques could, using stereoscopic coordinated camera shots, detect elevations and depressions in the surface of the land as small as six to twelve inches.

The plane came in from the east, flying at one thousand feet. The cameras were aligned and as they crossed over Northport Drive and flew almost directly down Troy Drive, the street leading to the hospital grounds, Professor Scherz began taking pictures. As they came in over the grounds, they could see the administration and treatment buildings. To the left they could see Governor's Island. They flew a straight line down Troy Drive, across the grounds, and headed off over the high point of the ground to the left of Goodland Hall. The plane then curved to the left, then came back and took a further series of photos on a line approximately two hundred feet south of their original approach. This time they were flying from the west and they took pictures of the grounds that contained the three eagle effigies and Governor's Island until they flew almost directly down Woodward Drive. The homes on the south side of that street were lakefront properties.

The plane turned one more time and they came back about another two hundred feet south and took pictures of the shoreline and Governor's Island. The plane then made a final swing to the right, arched up, and took pictures of the northernmost part of the land not known to have mounds. These shots included parts of Stovall Hall and most of Central Wisconsin Center, a hospital for developmentally disabled adults. The weather was perfect. Professor Scherz was sure that he and his students had the pictures they wanted.

The professor and his students were quite excited as they developed the Mendota photographs. Once developed they pored over them, noting from past surveys and drawings that had been made available to them, the places where there were clear changes in the terrain. It was not difficult for them to see and outline the major mounds groups. The three eagles of the central cluster were particularly evident, as were the panther and the bear mounds. The conical mounds on the highest point of the land in the western cluster were also clear. There was also evidence of a number of linear mounds that had been noted in previous drawings and surveys but which were difficult to see on the ground, principally because of erosion. Of even more interest, however, was the detectable evidence of a deer mound just north of the left wing of the largest eagle effigy. This deer was clearly noted to have four legs, as previous surveys had shown, and it was with satisfaction that Professor Scherz was able to note, looking into the forested area where this mound was, that there was still definition to its form.

The survey maps were completed by adding the contour lines showing changes in elevation. On reexamining them, Professor Scherz was surprised to note that an east-west line connected the principal burial mound on the highest point of the grounds with the eagles. It passed between the tips of the wings of the two great eagles and appeared to lie directly in line with the bottom of the feet of the four-legged deer.[1] What to make of such a connection, however, was not yet clear. But that such a connection could and would have meaning would not be surprising, especially if one was aware that such patterns and meaningful connections could be found in the works of other master builders. For instance, when Michelangelo was asked to renovate Capitoline Hill in Rome he used a simple isosceles triangle to connect "old Rome" with the "new Rome of Christendom."[2]

Capitoline Hill, one of the legendary seven hills of Rome, rises up from the Roman forum, to the southeast. (See Figure 4.) On top of this hill, the one closest to the forum, Michelangelo used the new city hall as a base and then altered two buildings of equal length on either side of the city hall to form a "square" between them and the base. Close observation however reveals that these buildings are not parallel to each other but slope toward each other so that if they were extended away from Capitoline Hill they would meet in the distance to form an isosceles triangle, i.e. a triangle with two equal sides. He sculpted the land to form a rise in the center of the "square" and on the rise he placed a newly found statue of Marcus Aurelius, the Roman Emperor known for his philosophical views. The statue had been well known in antiquity and had recently been found in the mud of the Tiber River. The statue consisted of Marcus Aurelius dressed as an emperor, seated on a horse, right arm extended and pointing forward. This statue was placed so that Marcus Aurelius pointed to the apex of the triangle.

Now, of interest to us is that the apex of the projected triangle lies across the city, on the dome of St. Peters Bascilica, the new seat of power. In this construction, old Rome represented by the forum and "City Hall" of Capitoline Hill point through a Roman Emperor who struggled to recognize Christianity as a permitted religion, to the new Rome or the Vatican. This simple geometric arrangement, with the addition of a single statue, was a symbolic

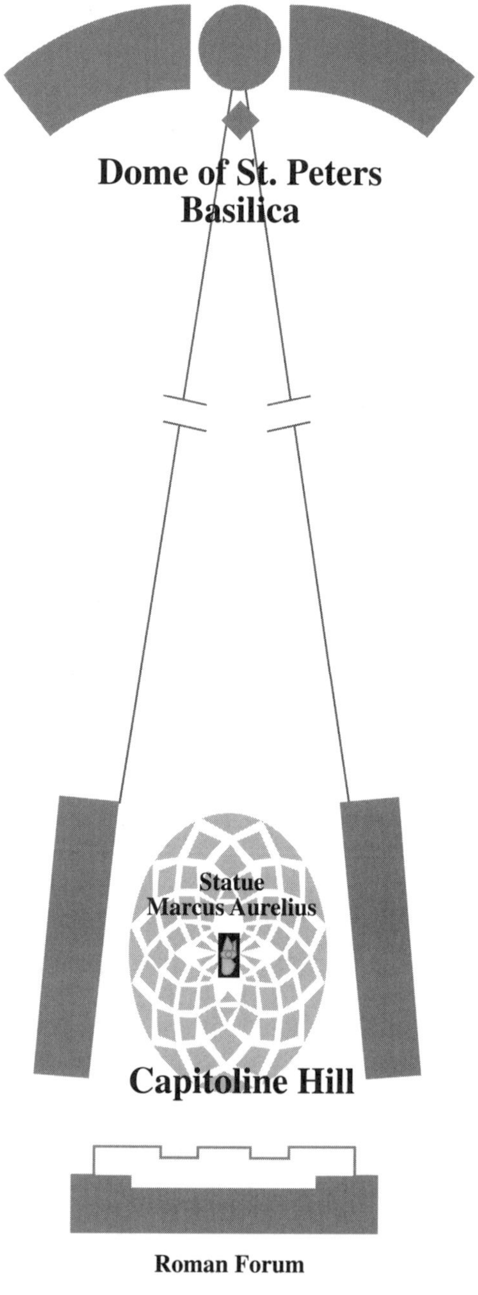

**Dome of St. Peters
Basilica**

**Statue
Marcus Aurelius**

Capitoline Hill

Roman Forum

Figure 4. Michelangelo's renovation of Capitoline Hill, Rome.

way to unite two powerful Roman worlds, the Rome of the Caesars and the Rome of the Popes. This construction is an example of an alignment, the kind the builders of the mounds used consistently in their constructions.

In our construction, however, it was not until Professor Scherz and his students had walked the grounds, confirming physically the meaning of the changes in the contour of the land, that his final maps, as published in the summer of 1985, showed that such alignments were completed. First, he was able to demonstrate that the effigy turtle mound, the one instructing me, had a meaningful alignment. It aligned to the major standstill of the moonset. While this is a mouthful of words, the meaning of the alignment will become understandable with the following explanation.[3] (See Figures 5 to 8.) The sun and the moon both appear to rise in the east, journey across the sky, and set in the west. While it appears that they are moving, we now know that the illusion of their movement reflects the rotation of the earth. At the same time as they make an east-to-west arc across the sky, from one horizon to the other, they also appear to an observer looking east as they rise, to move from day to day on the eastern horizon north or south, depending on the time of year. For the sun, the movement forms an arc starting in the northeast to a spot in the southeast, from the summer solstice through the fall equinox to the winter solstice. The sun then moves day to day back through the same arc, from the shortest day of the year, to the spring equinox, to the summer solstice, the longest day of the year. The sun's movement on the horizon as it rises in the east maps out the solar year. Similarly, when the sun sets it also describes a specific arc on the western horizon from the summer solstice, through the fall equinox, and on to the winter solstice, and then back. For a given latitude the sun moves through a specific number of degrees north and south of the equator. And it is at the periods when the sun approaches a maximum that it appears to slow down, stop, and then reverse itself, that it looks as if it is standing still on the horizon. This process is called the solstice, Latin for sun (sol) and standstill (stice). This happens in both the summer and the winter.

There are also two days each sun year when the sun is at the midpoint, called the equinox, and those are days when there is equinox, literally equal night, that is the light and the dark of the day-night

CARDINAL DIRECTIONS

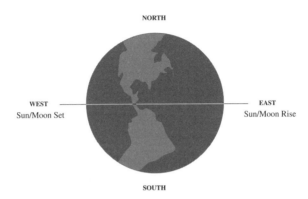

Figure 5. The sun and moon appear to rise in the east and set in the west.

SUNRISE, ONE SOLAR YEAR

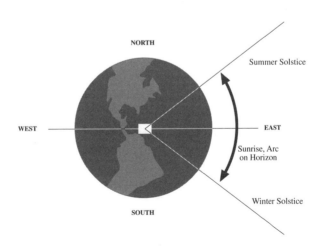

Figure 6. The sun, in rising over the period of a year, describes an arc on the eastern horizon as it moves from the summer solstice to the winter solstice and back again.

SUNSET, ONE SOLAR YEAR

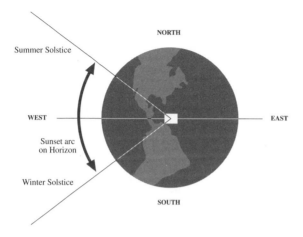

Figure 7. In like manner, the sun describes and arc on the western horizon as it sets during the year.

SUNRISE/SUNSET, ONE SOLAR YEAR

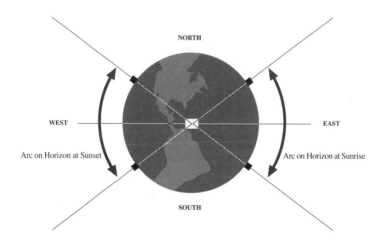

Figure 8. For any given latitude, the sun has fixed markers on the horizon for the longest and shortest days of the year.

cycle are equal. These of course occur in the spring and fall. The summer solstice is the longest day of the year and is usually around June 21st. The winter solstice is the shortest day of the year and is usually around December 21st. Natural people lived within the cycle of this day-night process and in telling seasonal time became as familiar with the position of the sun on the horizon as a way to measure the yearly cycle as we do by looking at a calendar.

While many cultures use the sun's movement as the basis for their calendar, other cultures use the moon. We may in fact remember that the word *month* comes from the word *moon*. In any given solar year there are approximately thirteen cycles of the moon or "months," each lasting twenty-eight and one-half days. But each culture has had to decide whether it would use the sun or the moon to regulate its "annual" calendar. The Babylonians, Egyptians, Romans, and Christians all adopted the sun as their standard. The

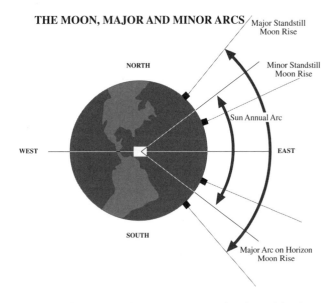

THE MOON, MAJOR AND MINOR ARCS

Major Standstill Moon Rise

Minor Standstill Moon Rise

NORTH

Sun Annual Arc

WEST

EAST

SOUTH

Major Arc on Horizon Moon Rise

Figure 9. In 18.61 solar years, the moon moves back and forth across the horizon, forming a major arc with a major standstill, to a minor arc and a minor standstill. It then moves back to the major standstill. These also provide fixed markers on the horizon which are specific for a given latitude.

Jews, Mayans, Aztecs, and Chinese also incorporate the movement (but not the phases) of the moon.

The moon has a different pattern of movement at the horizon. (See Figure 9.) The sun describes a single complete arc from the northwest position in the summer through the equinox to a southwest position in the winter and then back to the northwest position in one year. The moon completes a cycle that is 18.61 sun years long. It has a major arc and a minor arc. While this may be more than can be understood right now, the important point is that Professor Scherz was able to demonstrate that the long axis of the turtle had a meaningful orientation to an actual celestial body, the moon, at a meaningful time in its arc, its maximum standstill. This then not only added significance to the geometric construction of the mounds but it did not conflict with the interpretation of the imagery that my son had given me in the dream. In fact, it did not take long to recognize that the turtle's alignment to the moon connected the moon with the sun. Since the moon possesses no light of its own; what it does is reflect the sun's light. If the sun actually died when it set, its light would not be "available" to light objects like the moon. The ancients and so Native Americans, too, concluded that the sun was still shining once it set, even though it was out of sight below the horizon. The moon, in reflecting the sun's light, became a witness to the continuing presence or existence of the sun. If the turtle mound were alive, it could share the fact that even though the sun had set, and was below the surface of the earth, it was still shining. Why? because the moon reflects its "living" light. This observation was quite innervating because when combined with other such observations it formed a consistent pattern: alignments to the moon told us to look for the sun. The moon leads to the sun because the moon reflects the sun's light. Such patterns became part of the syntax of the earth writing of the mounds and supported the contention that the mounds were a language system.

There were other exciting alignments discovered as a result of the survey. The next obvious one was that if you drew an east-west line through the largest conical mound, it passed almost equidistance between the tips of the wings of the two large eagles on the grounds to the east. Even more interesting, the four-legged deer mound appeared to be standing on that line. In an uncanny way, the east-west line drawn through the conical mound directly to the east passed right along the bottom of the feet of this four-legged deer. Surely this was intended and not a chance relationship. A third interesting feature became evident. In an attempt to discover why the Indians laid out the eagle effigies in the position that they did, Professor Scherz, once he had the survey correct, took a line north, not magnetic north, but a line north off of the point near the north star, that is the celestial north. He drew a line through the place in the largest eagle where the long axis of the wings met at right angles to the long axis of the body. Through that intersection point he drew a line up to the heavens and then he measured the angle from that line to the body of the bird, it was 43 degrees. Forty-three degrees is the latitude of Madison. The city is 43 degrees north of the equator. Such were the fascinating relationships that came out of the professor's lab, that I still remember the wonder I felt one noon as I drove home from a class with Scherz and his students.

Professor Scherz knew from previous surveys that the Indians had aligned mounds not only with the solstice and equinox points of the sun and moon on the horizon, but also to form angular relationships with the north star.[4] It became quite clear that there was one meaningful reason why the largest eagle mound was placed in its particular position. It had coded in it a relationship with the North Star, a star navigators still use to guide them, that described the angle of the latitude of Madison. The fact that the smallest eagle flying in parallel was positioned in the same way meant it had the latitude coded in it, too. And considering that eagles fly, it was not surprising therefore that a meaningful alignment was found "in the sky," with the North Star. When compared to the fact that the turtle was pointed down the hill and had an alignment with a setting moon, further clues to the syntactical relationship of the mounds as a language system began to present themselves.

Let us now explore how this might be shared with children, remembering that transcultural issues are hard to explain to adults. The lack of life experience is, of course, a limiting factor for children, but adapting the subject matter to their mindset can allow them to make relevant associations.

Chapter V

EDUCATION
Teaching by Example

T hou art everywhere, but I worship you here;
   Thou art without form, but I worship you in these forms;
   Thou needest no praise, yet I offer you these prayers
and salutations.

— Hindu Prayer

If you wish to make an apple pie truly from scratch, you must
first invent the universe.

— Carl Sagan

The days were crisp, the skies overcast. The sun, moon, and stars
were occasionally visible. In the fall of each school year students
in grades four and five in Wisconsin study Native American cultures.
For a number of years, using slides, I have shared my understanding of the purpose of the mounds as part of a presentation to classes
at various schools in Madison. The following is a typical presentation to a class of nine- and ten-year olds:

Kids, it is my honor this afternoon to share some observations
about the Native American Indians who lived in this area as they relate
to the Indian mounds that are still present in Madison. One day the
Indians will teach this themselves. While they are still recovering from
the effects of the wars that the European culture inflicted on them,
ending with a massacre at Wounded Knee, South Dakota, over a hundred years ago, their cultural traditions are reviving and growing
stronger.[1] They are progressively ready to take on the teaching of their

heritage. It is with this respect that I share some impressions of their way of life and one of their legacies, the mounds.

Human beings have buried their dead in graves for perhaps fifty thousand years. Most of us know that when a person dies in our culture, she or he is typically placed in a coffin that is then buried six feet underground. You know that on the grave we place a gravestone that has the name of the person and the years they were born and died. A loving message related to the deceased person is often included on the stone. The slide I am showing you here is my mother's grave. See how simple her gravestone is? The story I want to share about the mounds that are on the grounds at the Mendota Mental Health Institute here in Madison has to do with an Indian burial. Before we can come to understand this, however, we have to understand a little bit about the mounds in general.

There are two types of mounds. The first type are burial mounds. Burial mounds come in two kinds, those shaped like heaps of dirt on the ground called conical mounds, and those sculpted in long straight lines, called linear mounds. Conical mounds could have up to six people buried in them. Linear mounds might only contain artifacts and no burials, or they could be mass graves and have up to thirty people buried in them.

The second type of mounds are called effigy mounds because they are sculpted to look like pictures of animals. Effigy is a French word which means picture, or portrait. How many of you have dogs as pets? How many cats? How about fish, birds? Anybody have turtles, snakes? Ah ha. Anybody ever take a picture of their pets? Sure, I'll bet at show-and-tell in first grade some of you brought in your pets. Right. Right!!!

Our culture tends to see animals in one of two ways: as pets, like the kind you have at home, and as food, like the hamburgers and fish fillets we get at McDonald's. With our advanced technology we no longer depend on animals to do our work, but we remember that they used to share their power with us, right? How do we measure the power of a car? Sure, we say it has so much horsepower, because before we had machines, horses did a lot of work for us. We do not understand, or we have lost our understanding, of animals as beings with special senses, as helpers to guide us. Furthermore, we have not only reduced animals to the two classifications of pets and food, but we have reduced the larger dimension of animals as symbols of transcendence, to one dimensional signs as mascots of school teams or as advertising or cartoon figures. Who is this? Right, Wiley Coyote. Does Wiley Coyote ever catch the Road Runner? No, he doesn't. Does Mighty Mouse ever fail? No. Even Walt Disney has done some animals a disservice by vilifying them. Who were the bad guys in *The Lion King*? The hyenas, right? I wonder how they felt about that.

Who is this? Right, Bucky Badger. Bucky Badger is the University of Wisconsin–Madison team mascot. He's one tough badger, right? What is this a picture of? Of course, it's the American Eagle. The American Eagle is on every American dollar bill. The American Eagle is a special bird that became endangered by our culture and is now protected and recovering. Let's start by looking at an aerial view of the eagle effigy mounds on the grounds of Mendota. See here. This picture was taken after one of the last snowfalls in the spring and you can see that the snow has melted off the south side of the mound leaving the snow outlining the north side of the eagle mound. Obviously these three eagles were important to the people that built them, but they were not just pets or food. They had more than the symbolic nature of the eagle on the American dollar. They were a totem animal that had spiritual significance, animals as symbols that would help the members of that animal clan get to the Happy Hunting Grounds. They would help each clan member to enter the great mystery. Sounds different, right?

Now look over here farther west on the grounds of Mendota. See the little black circles on this map? These are conical mounds. Here is a picture of the conical mound from the side. See how it arches up? It is flattened on top because this was one that was excavated in 1876 by Dr. DeHarte, the superintendent of the Mendota State Hospital. This is the view from the north looking south that shows the best preserved look of this conical burial mound as a mound. What are these? Pyramids, of course. And what are pyramids? Right, they are stone structures. Who were they for? For the Pharaohs. Right, for important people. Inside this burial mound was a stone chamber and inside the stone chamber three people were buried. You could think of each conical mound as a separate pyramid, each of which contained people who had died or artifacts for the journey to the afterworld. We know that the Egyptians believed in an afterworld and that is why they built the pyramids, not as monuments to the dead but as places where the physical remains of the dead could be kept intact while the spirit of each person, their soul, traveled to heaven.

The American Indians, too, believed in an afterlife. They believed in the Happy Hunting Grounds. They believed in the Great Spirit. The Sioux called the Great Spirit *Wankan Tanka*. Other American Indian Nations used other words to describe the Great Spirit. The Great Spirit was neither a man nor a woman. The Great Spirit was a mystery. The totem animal of each clan was a guide to help the Indians maintain contact or communicate with the Great Spirit.

The eagle mounds on the grounds of Mendota were built by members of the Eagle Clan, just as the three bears on the golf course at the Blackhawk Country Club were doubtless built by the Bear Clan. There is no doubt that the effigy mounds—remember that effigy is a French word meaning picture or portrait—were portraits of the animal that a particular clan had chosen to identify with. We have a remnant of that in our Boy Scouts and Girl Scouts. Cub Scout packs are sometimes named after animals.

Here is the drawing that Dr. DeHarte left us, showing the way that three people were buried in this grave.[2] (See Figure 10.) See, there is one adult skeleton here at the top. It appears to be in a sitting position. Here is the head and the chest. Here is the upper arm, called the humerus, and the lower part of the arm apparently placed in the lap. These are the bones of the legs in the front. See directly below the first adult, another adult. Their backs are almost perfectly aligned in the grave. Then look behind the adult seated in the bottom of the grave. There is a smaller skeleton that was thought to be a child six to eight years old. It is seated on the same physical plane as the adult on that level. So the burial contained three people, two adults and a child. Dr. DeHarte couldn't tell whether these were men or women. He couldn't tell what they died of. He said that he sent the bones to the Smithsonian Institution in Washington. I have tried to locate them but they don't have any record of having received these particular skeletons.[3]

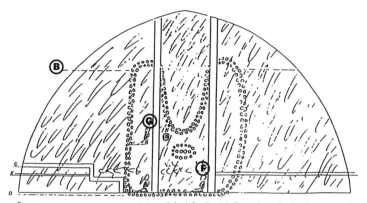

DESCRIPTION AND ORDER OF THE BURIALS.—A. Perpendicular shaft. D and E. Groups of stones found by the excavators 5 feet, below summit; next a layer of yellow clay about 4 feet deep. C, a drift made into the side ; feet above the ground K. D. bottom of the mound consisting of a bed of yellow clay. G, skeleton with perforated humerus, pieces of pottery and a stone implement. H, stones, ashes, charcoal and decayed wood. F, two skeletons, one of a child six years old, the other of an adult; found with pieces of pottery and two stone implements, 1 ½ feet below the surface of the ground.

Figure 10. The burial mound on the grounds of the Mendota Mental Health Institute in Madison, Wisconsin, excavated by Dr. DeHarte in 1876. The stone chamber marked "B" contained three skeletons—two adults under "G" and a child at "F."

Let me tell you how they buried them. First they dug down into the earth. They then laid a stone base, perfectly flat, and then around the edge they started to build a stone wall, like the walls of a house. See, there are two rows of stones and as they built up the stone walls, they placed the dead people in the position they wanted them buried. Sometimes they were placed lying down. In this particular case they were placed in a seated position. Sometimes they were clothed and sometimes they were not. Once they had the person in the position that they wanted them in, they packed them in dirt. They built the grave from the bottom up, packing the people in dirt and then creating any artifacts, like this ball of stones, in the middle of the grave. They then built the walls all the way up, finally placing the third person, the second adult, in perfect alignment with the adult below. They then finished the chamber by closing it with two rows of stones. Around the stones they molded wet clay until the exterior was smooth. Next, they placed a bonfire over the whole grave, which baked the clay and sealed the grave. They then took the dirt that they had excavated and placed it back around the stone chamber until they molded the shape they desired. Finally they packed special or sacred soil brought in from sacred places, like the Dells, over the whole surface.

Sometimes they planted special grasses on the top of the effigy mound. The special grasses were a different color and grew taller than the local grasses so that they could be seen by anybody passing by. The highways of the time weren't like the roads we travel on, they were the lakes and rivers. Traveling on the lakes and rivers was faster and easier than traveling on the land. Anyone canoeing on Lake Mendota or walking on the old Indian trail that is still on our grounds, would have been able to see these mounds because the grass on the mound was taller than the local grass and of a different color. Isn't that interesting?

Have any of you had anybody in your family die? *A number of hands go up.* Anybody's grandparents? How would you feel if somebody decided that they wanted to know how they had died and decided to dig up your grandparents? Would that be OK? No? Neither are the Native American Indians happy that anthropologists and archaeologists have an interest in digging up the graves of their grandparents. At the time that Dr. DeHarte excavated this grave there were no rules to protect the mounds, there were only the ethics of each investigator. And since it was his belief that these were ancient graves, he didn't feel he was disturbing known ancestors of the Ho-Chunk. Now all the mounds are protected by a Wisconsin law called the Burial Sites Act. These graves cannot be excavated or disturbed without a thorough review. If a mound is a burial mound, it cannot be disturbed. If it is not a burial mound, it sad to say, may be "disturbed." But in general the mounds have the protection of the law and the respect that they deserve.

Now let's look at one more set of relationships here. How many people were buried in the grave? Three. How many adults? Two. How many children? One. How many big people? Two, the adults. How many little people? One, the child. Let's look now over at these eagles. How many big eagles are there? Two. How many little ones? One. Remember how the people were buried in the grave? Uh huh, the one adult above the lower adult and the child behind the lower adult. Right. Look at how these eagles are laid out. The smallest eagle is flying parallel with the largest eagle. If those birds were to fly, they would fly together. They would reach the same destination. Like this child and this adult on the same level at the bottom of the grave. Now look here at the eagle mounds. Above and to the right we have the second largest eagle. Just as in the grave, it was above, but not to the right. So the three effigy eagle mounds have the same number, the same size, and the same relative positions as the three people in the grave.

Remember my mother's gravestone? The writing on my mother's gravestone identified who she was and the year of her birth and death. It has become clear to those of us who have studied the Indian Mounds that the effigy mounds that were close to the burials were the earth writing that contained the same information that we put on our gravestones. In other words, the three eagle effigy mounds identify the number of people that were buried in that grave and they identify that they are from the Eagle Clan because they were made as eagles and not as bears or foxes. They also show how the people were buried. This conclusion is easier to draw when we note the following connection between the cluster of conical mounds and the eagle effigy mounds. This east-west horizontal line drawn through the principal conical mound, that is the mound that Dr. DeHarte excavated, goes right through the tips of the wings of the two large eagles. This equinox line, in the language of mounds earth-writing, says that these two things are equal. Just as on an equinox day there is equal light and dark, things that are placed on an east/west, equinox line, are thought to be equal, or the same, or in harmony, or balanced, or symmetrical. These are the associative ideas that are connected with such an alignment. So, joining the conical mounds with an equinox line to the tips of the wings of two largest eagle effigies says that members of the Eagle Clan buried three Eagles, two adults and a child, in a specific position in that grave.

There is one other interesting observation that can be made from this aerial survey map. Look closely now at the deer effigy mound. (See Figure 11.) See how it is lying flat on the ground with its feet pointing north? How many feet does the deer have? Not sure...? Well let's look at a 1906 survey of this particular mound. Here we have this mound just as it is positioned on the survey map, with its feet pointing north, and there are how many—yes, four feet. What is important about this particular mound is that it differs from other mounds of animals with four legs. When the builders of the mounds depicted a four-legged animal, they usually put one appendage at the front representing two legs and one appendage at the back representing the back two legs. For some reason they put four legs on this deer, two in the front and two in the back. This deer was so unusual that it was studied by different groups from the mid-1880s on. They were able to confirm, as this survey in 1906 did, that the deer did in fact have four legs.

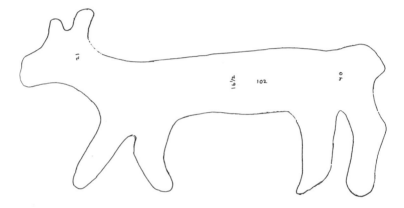

Figure 11. The four-legged deer effigy mound was surveyed by A. B. Stout on July 29, 1906. The deer is 102 feet from nose to tail, 16½ feet across the body, and 40 feet from the back to the bottom of the hind legs. The deer had antlers but because of erosion there was no evidence that the antlers were bifurcated.

There was another interesting feature of this deer mound that the writer of the 1906 survey noted. See the deer's antlers? It was thought by earlier investigators that this deer had bifurcated antlers. They thought the antlers branched out into different points. We will come to that in a minute. The surveyor of 1906 said that while he could confirm that the deer had four legs, he could not confirm that the antlers were bifurcated. He attributed this to erosion.

Do any of you know what happens to the antlers of a male deer in winter? They fall off. That's right. Each spring a male deer grows new antlers. The older the deer, the more points in the antlers. Have any of your fathers or mothers gone deer hunting? Yes, a number.

Don't they get excited when they tell their friends that they shot a five-, six-, or seven-point buck. A rack of antlers that has five, six, or seven points on each side would indicate a truly wise old animal.

Native peoples around the world understood that when a thing dies, something new will come to life, like when a tree dies in the forest, mushrooms and other things will grow out of it. Any animal that had a cyclic change in its body that was related to the solar year, such as the deer with its antlers, became a symbol of death and rebirth.[4] Let me say this another way. Does anybody know what happens to the skin of a snake each year? Anybody? That's right, it falls off. Snakes shed their skin. Snakes are thought to be sacred animals by most cultures because they shed their skin every year and appear to be reborn, or to grow again. In fact, in nearly every culture except those whose religions started with Abraham, that is the Jews, Christians, and Moslems, the snake is revered. It is a sacred symbol. Two snakes which cross each other seven times, called the caduceus, is the symbol of health of doctors. Can anybody remember what happened to the snake in the Garden of Eden? That's right, the snake told Eve to tell Adam to take a bite of the apple and because she and Adam did, the snake and everyone else was kicked out of the garden. Anybody Catholic here? Okay. Do you know what happened to the snake in the Catholic Church? That's right. The Blessed Virgin subdued the snake. She is usually shown in statue form stepping on the head of the snake. The snake, a symbol of health for nearly every other culture, turned out to be a symbol of the devil for the Jews, Christians, and Moslems. Actually, as modern feminist research has shown, the snake was one symbol of the ancient goddess. The one-male-God religions started by Abraham conquered the goddess and in the process the symbols of the goddess, including the snake, that used to be sacred became associated with the devil, and evil.[5] Kinda sad, right?

Do you know what people think about as they grow old? No? OK, well, their thoughts often turn to the question of life after death. And they sometimes start to practice "religion." They start to use the symbols of death and rebirth to strengthen their belief in an afterlife. Natural peoples around the world identified with animals that shed their skin, shed their antlers, or like the male peacock, shed their feathers, in the annual cycle. They thought they were special animals that had special power to give meaning and direction to the afterlife, to the afterworld, to the Great Spirit. So this deer was special because it had four legs and because it had antlers. And we know it was a two-point buck because Reverend Peet, who drew the first diagram of these mounds, also made a separate drawing of this deer showing the four legs and two pointed antlers, which he published later in 1890.

Now that we have made the connection between the three eagle effigy mounds and the three people that were buried in the tomb, let's consider the alignment of the largest eagle effigy and its smaller companion. We have seen from the aerial photograph, which was later confirmed by the aerial survey, that they are flying together. They are flying in formation. They are flying parallel to each other. Why were they placed in that particular position? Since birds fly, perhaps something in the sky might have a bearing on it. Most of us know that the North Star, called Polaris, is used by navigators, captains of ships, and planes, to navigate on clear nights. The North Star is in that position in the sky around which all the other stars appear to turn in one year. The North Star can be found if you know the position of the Big Dipper. It is four times the distance between the last two stars in the cup of the Big Dipper, projected out from the bottom of the dipper. I know that is complicated, but if we were to stand on the place where the axis of the body and the axis of the wings of the great eagle intersect, if we were to stand on that spot, right here on this slide, and draw a line up to the North Star, we would create an angle between the North Star and the body of the bird. That's this angle right here. (See Figure 12.) That angle, in our system of measurement, is 43 degrees. Forty-three degrees has special significance for Madison. Does anybody know what it is? Has anybody here heard of longitude or latitude? Okay. Latitude is the number of degrees a place is north of the equator. Madison is 43 degrees north of the equator.

While that might sound complicated, there is another way to say it. If you want to know your relationship to the North Star, go out at night and look up at the North Star. In Madison you will be looking up at a 43-degree angle. Forty-three degrees is the angle between the horizon and the North Star. The latitude of any place north of the equator is simply the angle to the North Star. Let's try one more way of

NORTH STAR ALIGNMENT

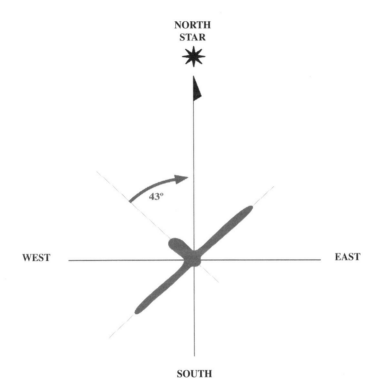

Figure 12. The angle between the body of the eagle and the North Star form a 43-degree angle.

thinking of this. If you were a stick figure and you were at the North Pole, where would you find the North Star? That's right, directly overhead. You would be standing on the earth, looking straight ahead, and your head would have to turn up ninety degrees to be able to look up at the North Star. When Professor Scherz completed his aerial survey, not only did he find that the turtle aligned with the major standstill of the moon and that an equinox line connected the burial mound with the eagles, but he was able to determine that a line off the North Star through that point in the eagles, marked the latitude. These two eagles were placed on the ground to mark the latitude. A person with an understanding of how to read the language of the mounds would know to look for that particular relationship. In the language of earth writing, this was their way of saying that the eagles knew what their relationship was to the North Star, and on their journey to heaven they used that alignment to indicate that they wanted to have a relationship with that spot, the immovable spot in the heavens, the spot that appears not to move, the spot that all the other stars seem to move around. Neat hey?

Yes it is neat when considering these relationships through the eyes of children. Let us now consider the meaning that might result when the same relationships are fit into a more sophisticated context. While the basic relationships will remain constant, the background against which they will be interpreted will require some knowledge of history, architecture, and sculpture. It will also require some awareness of the basic tenets of Christian theology. However, what the reader is not familiar with, the text will explain. Finally, the wisdom of age will also help us integrate the many levels of meaning intended in the construction.

Chapter VI

EDGEWOOD RETREAT
Resurrecting Old Spirits

I*n the life of the Indian, there is only one inevitable duty—the duty of prayer—the daily recognition of the unseen and eternal. He sees no need for setting apart one day in seven as a holy day, since to him all days are God's.*

— Ohiyesa, Santee Dakota

If spirit is completely transcendent, it is also completely imminent. I am firmly convinced that if a new and comprehensive paradigm is ever to emerge, that paradox will be its heart.

— Ken Wilber

A group of Dominican Sisters decided to spend a week retreat at Edgewood College in Madison to acquaint themselves with the spirituality of the Ho-Chunk as it related to the effigy mounds. They had picked a sunny, warm week in early June 1992 for their retreat/workshop. They asked me to present my research findings of the Mendota mounds and to include in the presentation my comparison of the theology of the Medici Chapel with the "liturgical" afterdeath statement implied in the burials on the grounds of the Mendota Mental Health Institute. Sister Barbara Beyenka, the nun in charge of organizing the workshop, was aware that I was a "recovering Catholic" and that on my faith journey I had developed a relationship with a turtle spirit helper. She was aware that I had given the place I had formerly dedicated to my guardian angel to Nottwo, the turtle. Her broad ecumenical orientation to this spirit was refreshing throughout the presentation.

Following is the talk that I presented that day:

Sisters, first let me thank you for inviting me to share my growing understanding of the mounds with you this afternoon. Let me
then present a brief summary and general overview of the burial and
effigy mounds on the grounds of the Mendota Mental Health Institute. First, we have the documented evidence left by Dr. DeHarte
of the excavation. He showed how two adults and a child were
buried in the stone tomb located in the largest conical mound. They
were buried in a seated position facing west. The two adults were
buried aligned, one above the other. The child was buried behind
the lower adult on the same linear plane. We have also seen from
the aerial survey of Professor Scherz that the turtle effigy mound is
aligned with the major standstill of the moon. We have seen that an
equinox line drawn through the burial mound, eastward, goes
through the tips of the wings of the two large eagles, connecting
them, and that we have interpreted the three eagles to be the effigies, that is the actual portraits of the three people buried, the two
adults and the child, since the two large eagles and the small eagle
are the same in number, size and relative positions. We have seen
that they laid out the largest eagle and the small eagle in parallel
and that they describe a special relationship with the North Star,
marking their location's latitude. But more, we also note that the
eagles, who are on their journey to the Great Spirit, knew the earthly
relationship of this place on earth with the North Star, the star that
is placed near the center of the fixed place in the heavens, around
which all the stars appear to rotate each year. Finally, we have noted
that a special four-legged deer effigy is walking on the equinox line.
To date we have not been able to account for the alignment of the
second largest eagle. Consider then the following Ho-Chunk liturgy
and commentary I came across in 1988 in a book by Brotherston[1]
and my excitement when I discovered that Radin describes the same
liturgy in even greater detail.

The text here was documented around 1910 by an "anthropol-
ogist" who said the Ho-Chunk in Wisconsin had told him these
words were said at the "funeral" of deceased "nobles." The text used
by the shaman was typical of those confided to the deceased during
a four-day wake, in which the deceased passed through the underworld before walking into the sky. The four-day journey itself could

be undertaken only after certain ritual tests and examinations, for which the deceased was also prepared. On the way he might be helped by the spirits of people killed by the shaman as a warrior in battle, though for this to work and not have adverse effects the shaman was not to exaggerate his prowess. The actual course of the journey in time and space corresponds to that described by Algonkquin shamans from their trances; and, more dramatically, with some cosmological narratives of Meso-America. As if referring to a well-known doctrine, this Ho-Chunk text alludes briefly but firmly to ritual stations. These are west to the setting sun, then down to the underworld and Herecgunina's lodge, east to the footprints of the day; and finally to the zenith, and the lodge of the Earthmaker at midday. These four "stations" were also thought of as doors that opened each day to a new part of the afterworld journey. So on the first day the soul proceeded to the west to the land of the setting sun. On the second day, having passed through the second door, the soul encountered Herecgunina, Lord of the Underworld. If the soul outwitted Herecgunina, the soul would proceed through the third door and follow the instructions given by the grandmother to find the footprints of brothers and sisters who had gone before him in order to join his relatives beyond the fourth door in the heart of heaven. Listen to the liturgy.

My grandchild, Earthmaker, is waiting for you in great expectation. There is the door to the setting sun. On your way stands the lodge of Herecgunina and his fire. Those who have come (the souls of brave men) from the land of the souls to take you back will touch you. There the road will branch off towards your right and you will see the footprints of the day on the blue sky before you. These footprints represent the footprints of those who have passed into life again. Step into the places where they have stepped and plant your feet into their footprints, but be careful you do not miss any. Before you have gone very far, you will come into a forest broken by open prairies here and there. Here, in this beautiful country, these souls whose duty it is to gather other souls, will come to meet you. Waiting on each side of you, they will take you safely home. As you enter the lodge of Earthmaker, you must hand to him the sacrificial offerings. Here the inquiry that took place in the first lodge will be repeated and answer in the same manner. Then he will say to you, All that your grandmother has told you is true. Your relatives are waiting for you in great expectation. Your home is waiting for you. Its door will be facing the midday sun. Here you will find your relatives gathered.

You can imagine my excitement when I discovered this liturgy. To this point in my journey to understand the mounds and in my "conversations" with Nottwo I had not found a description of an afterdeath journey that was relevant to the mounds nor that seemed to give any architecture to the afterdeath journey. This particular liturgy was not only plausible because of its Ho-Chunk origins, that is Indians indigenous from time immemorial to this area, but when considering that the souls must pass through four doors on this four-day journey to Earthmaker, it is not a stretch of the imagination to think that the "doors" are actually present in the way the mounds are constructed. Let me show you.

First, it is my opinion that the reason the people were buried in a sitting position facing due west was to indicate that they were facing the first door, that is the doorway to the land of the setting sun. They knew they would need to journey to the land of darkness, to the land of death, as a first step on their journey to their God. Second, a further meaning of the alignment of the turtle with the moon could be that it is pointing to the second door. Consider the mounds as a painting in which the artist must add depth and indicate a descent. As the liturgy and commentary state, the souls must descend into the fiery Lodge of Herecgunina where they will undergo trials. The sun is a fireball and the sun descends below the horizon of the earth in the west. Observe that the turtle is sculpted going down the hill and that if the turtle were to move, its projected destination would not only be to its natural habitat, the lakeshore, but below the lake and ultimately below the surface of the earth to the place where the sun, a fiery ball, would continue descending into the underworld. Since the turtle has the ability to go below the surface of the water, symbolically it could also go below the surface of the earth. Thus, the turtle not only has an alignment with the major standstill of the moon, which alignment would tell those on land that the sun is still in fact alive below the horizon—because the moon reflects the sun's light—but the turtle itself would be able to help the soul descend with the sun to the underworld.

Consider now that every major ancient religion or mythology, embracing the ideas of death and rebirth in the Middle East, has a story of the descent of a hero or heroine into Hades or into hell. According to Virgil, Aeneus was tested in the underworld before he co-founded Rome, the eternal city, with Romulus and Remus.[2] Demeter descended into Hades to save her daughter, Persephone.[3] In the *Divine Comedy*, Dante descended to the shores of hell, went through purgatory, and then ascended to the gates of heaven.[4] In fact, in the modern Apostles Creed of the Catholic Church does it not say that ". . . Christ was crucified, died, and was buried. He descended into hell and on the third day He arose again from the dead. He ascended into heaven. . . ." In Christian theology the Savior spent three days in hell before His ascent to heaven. Our liturgy talks of a four-day journey.

Thus the turtle guides the souls in their descent to the trials in the Lodge of Herecgunina. The trials awaiting the souls were dangerous contests and not similar to those the Christian soul suffers in purgatory. According to Catholic doctrine, purgatory is the place where the souls that are not yet ready for the presence of God are purged of their imperfections. While it is painful and strenuous, the souls nevertheless know that they will one day be worthy of the presence of God and thus they have hope. For the Indians, the tests of the underworld in the Lodge of Herecgunina were feats of strength and endurance. They were more like games of wit and physical skill than punishments. While dangerous, those who were prepared were expected to pass them.

If we consider then the four-legged deer we may get some clues about the third door. If we let this deer stand up it would appear to be walking. And as the liturgy says, off to the right one will see a field and then one will see the footprints of the brothers and sisters that have gone before them in the sky. First, there is a field to the right of the deer as it goes down to the lake. Second, it is my opinion that one reason that this deer was given four legs, whereas all traditional four legged effigy mounds had their front legs depicted by one appendage and their back legs depicted by a second, was to capture the idea of walking and footprints. I think this observation is credible because the word "footprints" is repeated four times in the liturgy, as though the deer had four feet.

Consider then that one is to discover in the sky the footprints of brothers and sisters who have gone before. These footprints would probably be stars. It is my contention that the second largest eagle, whose alignment we have yet to account for, in fact aligns to a specific Ho-Chunk constellation at a special time in the year. In 1993 I received a Sioux sky chart that described nine Sioux constellations of stars .[5] While the Sioux map of the stars was specifically applied to holy places in the Dakotas, including Harney Peak and Devils Tower, it included an alignment to a group of seven stars called the Pleides by the Greeks. According to the Greeks, the Pleides are the seven daughters of Zeus. For the Sioux the same group of stars were coincidentally called the Seven Little Girls. Since the liturgy calls one to follow the footprints of brothers and sisters (girls?) and the Sioux called the Pleides little girls, I took the fall equinox at sunrise, the key from the deer, and let the second largest eagle fly. It flew very close to the Pleides. If one allowed for the fact that the Pleides would have been at a different place in the sky at the time of construction (since the constellations move over the centuries) it is quite possible this eagle points to the Pleides and could give an approximate date of the mounds construction. But it is more than plausible to consider that the second largest eagle effigy mound was placed on the ground in such a way as to align with the seven stars of the Pleides. This would symbolically represent the third door of the liturgy and in conjunction with the four-legged deer, an animal itself imbued with the symbolism of rebirth, underline the importance of following the path in a strict manner, being careful not to "miss" any footprints.

As you can see from the liturgy, the fourth door is directly overhead; when the sun is at its zenith, its door will be facing the midday sun. This is a particularly difficult direction for earth sculptors to capture when they are working on the flat canvas of the earth. Nevertheless, I believe that the walking deer serves a second purpose. First, to emphasize the idea of footprints and to give the day and time of day to discover the alignment to the sisters, and second, as the deer walks on to point to the fourth door, as follows:

Around the western Great Lakes there are a number of pictographs that show a half-rainbow with a stick man walking on it. (See Figure 13.) This has symbolically been taken to indicate a

Figure 13. Pictographs in the Western Great Lakes Region show a stick man walking on a half-rainbow to meet the sun at its zenith at noon.

journey to heaven or a journey to the sky. In fact, I think as the turtle pointed to the spot in the horizon where the souls were directed to descend through the second door, the deer points to the spot on the horizon at sunrise where the souls would be taken to "get on the sun" and ride with it to the zenith, to the fourth door, where the sun would be at midday.

It is not surprising, therefore, that the archeological evidence and the survey evidence can combine with this particular liturgy to complete the theological composition. The souls have been buried with an expectation that they will go on a four-day journey to their Great Spirit, here called Earthmaker. They need spirit helpers such as the turtle and deer, to guide them on their journey. They are aware that symbolically it is a four-day journey and that the souls will pass through four doors where they will be tested. This liturgy, in its simplicity, is fairly sophisticated compared to the simple statement that we have for instance in the Apostles Creed. It is not, however, as sophisticated as the Tibetan Book of the Dead, which describes a forty-nine day journey from death to rebirth through three Bardo planes. But that for another time.

There is another way for Christians to understand this liturgy and the mounds construction as a more elaborate description of the events that the soul encounters after death. In order to demonstrate this I would like to compare it to the theological beliefs about the afterlife that underpinned Michelangelo's composition in the Medici Chapel.[6] As you know, Michelangelo lived from 1470 to 1564, primarily in Florence and in Rome, during the Renaissance. Renaissance is French for the time of rebirth. Michelangelo was not only a master painter and sculptor, but also a writer, poet, and architect. Furthermore, he lived at a time when literally new worlds were being discovered. He was 22 when Columbus set sail for China and returned to Europe with news of the Americas. He lived at a time when the Christian Church entered a stage of reformation. He was 39 when Martin Luther nailed his theses to the church door in Wittenberg. He lived at a time when papal authority was eroding in some areas and maturing in others. He was, it might be said, a religious skeptic and it is clear from his work that he was not bound by the traditions of the church. Having said that, he was also a theologian. Let me describe the story he told through seven silent statues in the Medici Chapel in Florence, remembering that we are comparing his metaphor of the transcendence of death to that of six silent effigy mounds. What both have in common is a story told through silent forms, the statues of Michelangelo, the mounds of the Eagle Clan. The difference between the two is that we do not have to interpret much of Michelangelo's story because scholars intimately familiar with the body of his work, including his letters and philosophical views, have been able to interpret what the composition meant to him and how it was to be understood. Until the Elders of the Ho-Chunk decide to share the exact meaning of the mounds with us, the following interpretation will have to suffice as a first approximation of the real meaning. I offer it to help us bridge the gap between Christian and Native-American theology.

The Medici Chapel is a small square mausoleum off the main Medici Church of San Lorenzo in Florence, Italy. On the north and south walls are the sarcophagi of two of the minor Medici Dukes. On the south wall, Giuliano dressed as a Roman Emperor, is seated above his sarcophagus. (See Figure 14.) He looks over his left shoulder at a statue of the Madonna, a mother and child, on the west wall. On top of his sarcophagus are two famous statues. The man is called "Day." The woman is called "Night." These two statues are separated as if to allow the soul of the entombed Giuliano to rise between them, past the effigy statue, and move up on its journey to heaven.

On the north wall in a parallel composition, Lorenzo sits above his sarcophagus. (See Figure 15.) Below him are two statues, a man called "Dusk" and a woman called "Dawn." Lorenzo, dressed as a philosopher, sits like Rodin's "thinker," chin on hand looking to his right to the same statue of mother and child on the west wall.[7] Giuliano and Lorenzo sit above symbols of cyclic time, Day and Night, Dawn and Dusk. Trapped in the cycles of time they ponder the question, is there life after death? And they look to a mother and child for an answer.

On the west wall Michelangelo sculpted a statue of a Madonna. (See Figure 16.) The serene face of the virgin looks down on her son, Jesus, who is seated facing away from his mother. His upper body and head are turned to the left as he nurses on the Virgin's breast. The mother and child are part of Michelangelo's answer to the question, is there life after death. Drawing on neo-Platonic ideas prevalent at the time, he let the symbol of a mother's love for her child, a creator who would never harm her creation, be the testament that life endures beyond apparent death. Why? According to Plato in the Phaedo, because the creator is in love with his/her creations s/he would not harm them even though during their "life cycle" they may need to go through vigorous transformations, physical death being one of them. But just as the Virgin will participate in the transforming states of her son's life, including his apparent death, the creator abides with us through the transforming stages of our lives, including our death. Both know of the state of existence after death.

On the east wall is a simple Christian alter. As in the medieval cathedrals, the alter was placed in the east so that the congregation would associate the rising of the morning sun which will transform night into day, death into life, with the rising of the newly consecrated, and therefore transformed, host as it is elevated over the priest's head during the mass. As the sun transforms night into day,

Figure 14. Medici Chapel, Tomb of Giuliano de' Medici.

Figure 15. Medici Chapel, Tomb of Lorenzo de' Medici.

Figure 16. Medici Chapel, Virgin and Child.

dark into light, the consecrated host, transubstantiated, that is changed by the priest in it substance, will, for believers, transform a soul blackened by sin into a soul beautified by grace. Thus the infant Christ is seated so that when he is finished breast-feeding he will turn and face the alter on the eastern side of the chapel and his ultimate fate, crucifixion. The crucified Christ, by dying to his earthly ego, completes salvation, fulfilling the theological intent that God so loved the world that he sent his beloved Son in the form of a man to die that we might live eternally with him in heaven. The way out of cyclic time to eternity according to the Christian account lies in following that path. Silent marble statues make the statement that love-encompassed crucifixion-resurrection is the way to eternity.

By using these silent statues, Michelangelo has woven the neo-platonic idea that love is the most enduring force, into the ancient symbolism of the four directions, to answer the eternal question that there is life after death. Further, since the chapel is also layered in meaning from the floor level where the souls are entombed in stone, through a middle area representing purgatory and a top layer, heaven, Michelangelo also intended that the souls would rise from the depths of hell (from the rocks in the basement, remember?) transcending the symbols of cyclic time, past the persona of their stone statue, their effigy, up through the middle realms of purgatory and into the highest realm of heaven, where they would abide forever in their spiritual form. Matter, life, mind, then spirit.

Let me summarize this beautifully integrated theology in order to make the comparison with the mounds clear. Michelangelo was saying that the souls of the Medici dukes, trapped in cyclic time as symbolized by statues Day and Night, and Dawn and Dusk, were seeking transcendence of the cycles of time through a belief in the love of the creator for its progeny, best symbolized by Plato as the love of a mother for her child. This Neo-Platonic idea is woven into the Christian idea that the route to eternal life lies in a surrender and adoration of the crucifixion of Christ in which He triumphed over death. The concept of time that was being transcended here was cyclic time evidenced by day and night, dawn and dusk. I submit to you that this is the same notion of time that concerned the builders of the mounds.

In a further construction of the mounds close to the burial site you will notice evidence of two long linear mounds that seem to point to a central area where in fact there used to be another relatively large, conical mound. These mounds were partially destroyed by hospital construction, but when Professor Scherz put these mounds back as they were prior to destruction, this was clearly an important construction. In fact, it could be considered an outdoor cathedral. Consider that many Christian churches have a cemetery located immediately adjacent to the church. The bodies of the dead are reposed in the cemetery, usually to the west of the church. The living sacrament or the living word is shared inside the church. The area on the flat land immediately east of the burial mounds contains a similar analogy.

Let me explain. This area was embraced by two long linear mounds that formed a unique angle of 103 degrees or double phi, that is double 51.5. Phi, or the golden mean, is relatively strange to Westerners, but it is the base of what is called sacred geometry.[8] (See Figure 17.) The Greeks, masters of geometry, had discovered that a straight line could be divided in such a way that a constant relationship could be formed between the two segments. This was much like the constant relationship between the circumference and the diameter of a circle. We are familiar with the formula $C = pi \times D$, where pi is the constant relationship between circumference and diameter. We also know that it is a constant with a value of 3.14. The Greeks were also concerned about the division of a line that would define the following proportion, the first part of the division would be to the second, that is A is to B, as the second would be to the sum of both parts, that is B is to $(A + B)$. That proportion would read mathematically as A is to B as B is to the sum of A+B. That proportion is another constant called phi, with a numerical value of 1.61. When a right angle triangle is made with the shorter line, A as the base and the longer line, B as the vertical, an angle of 51.5 degrees is created at the base A with the hypotenuse. This is the angle of phi. The relationship of rectangles with A as one side and B as the other, is specifically known as the golden section or the golden mean. These rectangles are found throughout all sacred geometry. They are found in Greek temples and in the Christian cathedrals of the Middle Ages.

PHI, GOLDEN MEAN

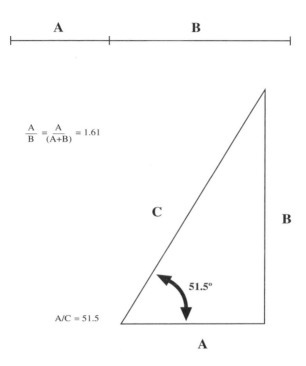

Figure 17. When a line is divided so that the proportion A:B as B:(A+B) is attained, a constant called Phi with a numeric value of 1.61 results. When a right-angled triangle is formed with A as the base and B as the vertical, an angle of 51.5 degrees is formed with the base.

They are found in Roman temples, Mayan temples, in the temples of India and at Ankor Wat, in Cambodia.

Of interest, then, is the fact that this aspect of phi, that is the expression of phi as an angle of 51.5 degrees, is found in sacred constructions. For instance, the Great Pyramid of Cheops rises from the base of each side to the apex at an angle of 51.5 degrees. Of further interest is that some ancient sacred places on the earth are at 51.5 degrees latitude or co-latitude, for instance Stone Henge is 51.5 degrees north of the equator. The major Native American Indian city in North America called Chahokia is located at the co-latitude of 51.5 degrees, i.e. 51.5 degrees south of the North Pole. The ancients realized that that particular relationship with the North Pole, which is also a relationship with the equator, was special and, therefore, it is not surprising that Professor Scherz has found the expression of phi as an angle in most major mounds constructions. Sometimes the angle is doubled, as it is here on the grounds of Mendota. But it is even more fascinating to consider that nature uses this proportion and angle in its constructions so frequently that phi is sometimes called the angle of life. Not only does the human body have this proportion embedded in relationships such as head, navel, and feet, but twigs grow from a branch in this proportion, a snail's shell grows out in 51.5 degree increments, and the DNA molecule rotates on a 51.5 degree turn. The ancients could not have known this last fact but the Hindus, for this very reason, put a conch shell in one of Shiva's hands to symbolize life. But enough of this digression.

Consider, then, this interesting relationship. (See Figure 18.) The two long linear mounds pointed to a conical mound now called the alter mound, that is the principal conical mound which would have been the center of the activity of any living ceremony that would have been conducted at this site. If one were to take a line from the North Star through that mound, it would bisect the angle between the long linear mounds, creating two angles of phi. It is quite clear that this division was purposeful. There are no conical mounds on the eastern side of the division of phi. The burial mounds and other conicals in the burial mound construction are all in the western expression of phi. This would indicate that the ceremonies of the living people would be conducted at this mound and bring "grace" from the heavens centered on the North Star, acting as an Axis Mundi, the axis connecting heaven and earth, to those people gathered on the eastern side of the plane. At the same time "graces" would be extended to the dead buried on the western side of phi. This is a way of saying that they believed that the activities of the living were important and could influence or affect those souls that had already passed on.

Let us now integrate this final construction into the whole western cluster of mounds as though they were analogous to a Christian church with a cemetery outside, thinking of this area as an open-air cathedral.[9] Consider that the souls have as their immediate

PHI, SACRED GROUNDS

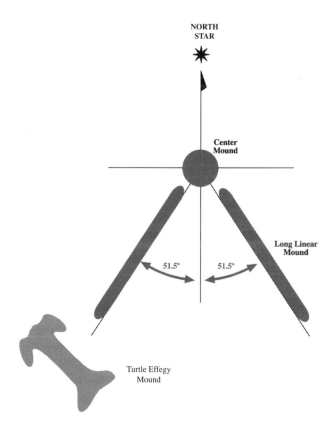

Figure 18. An imaginary line from the center mound to the north star bisects the two longest linear mounds, creating two angles or 51.5 degrees.

symbols of transcendence the sun and the moon. The turtle is aligned to the major standstill of the moon. The equinox line describes the rising and setting of the sun on special "equal" days. The sun and the moon are not only spheres but they are the principal means of measuring earthly time. The moon is the smaller cycle that grows from darkness (new moon) to fullness (full moon) and then ebbs to darkness so that in one lunar cycle there is birth, death and then rebirth. The sun measures the grander cycle of the year.

Both of these, however, are transitory. Both of these pass. Both of these are lost in a never-ending repetitive cycle. Measuring time by the cycles of the moon and the cycles of the sun is to be engulfed by cyclic time.

Christians celebrate the birth of Christ as the first cycle. We are now presently in the 2001st cycle, one after the other in a line, beginning with the birth of Christ. The Jews are in the 5,762nd cycle of the linear time of Abraham leaving the city of Ur. With the advent of counting these cycles, western culture changed from cyclic time to linear or historical time. We are engulfed in linear time. We live with the past, the present, and the future, with an expectation that with death our physical forms will end, but with a belief and hope that the part of ourselves that we feel is eternal, that we intuit is eternal, will in fact live on after our body has fallen away. Christian faith tells believers to believe in the resurrection of the body and life everlasting.

The conceptual time zone the mounds builders needed to transcend was cyclic time. Like the statues of Day and Night and Dawn and Dusk, which are symbols of cyclic time, they used the sun and moon, the most obvious symbols of cyclic time, to describe one aspect of their conception. However, they knew that there was a spot in the heavens that was fixed and immovable. The North Star is close to that spot. They, therefore, in their constructions used the North Star as the symbol of eternity. It was the immovable spot, the transcendent spot. It was the heavenly spot that was connected to the sacred places on the earth by the Axis Mundi. Whereas the sun at midday is the daytime symbol of the door to heaven, the North Star represents that spot at night. And because the sun continues to cycle across the sky by day and "dies" at night, the North Star at the center of the stars has therefore the dominant place in orienting spiritual energy because it is constant in the heavens.

Thus we find the orientation to the North Star as the critical final place in the composition, not just because the souls went on a four-day journey ending at the zenith in the heavens, but because the living could reach out and try to influence and relate to their ancestors by constructing earthly monuments in a meaningful relationship with the North Star. Further, the ceremonies that were conducted on this sacred site would have added spiritual energy to the meaning of the earth sculptors. But the Ho-Chunk lost "control" of this sacred site in the early 1800s. Since then the mounds have not only been unattended by their creators but many have been destroyed by the European invaders. The spiritual and cultural energy that used to be so powerful has grown cold. But with the mounds being protected as burials and with a growing recognition of the sophistication of their constructions, the spiritual energy of the mounds is in the process of recovering. More, the Ho-Chunk themselves now have resources they can dedicate to recovering their land. Then to add icing to this cake, the State Historical Society of Wisconsin has made real efforts to connect with the Ho-Chunk and other tribes to develop common goals and policies toward preserving and even promoting the mounds. This could lead to a fruitful conclusion that, if nurtured, the mounds as sacred sites could become again a source of healing and strength for people. If this happens, the spiritual energy will itself have gone through a cycle of death and rebirth, dying in the early 1800s and being reborn in the early 21st century. They could become "hot" again.

One common goal, therefore, of people interested in the mounds can be to protect them and then invite the Ho-Chunk to reclaim them, insofar as possible, to strengthen their culture. At the same time, bringing their spiritual dimension back to life in a way that our predominantly Christian population can appreciate is also part of "saving" the mounds and bringing back their power. Presentations like this help build these bridges and the base on spiritual understanding in a transcultural process. So I, and we, thank you for this opportunity to share these observations. Any questions?

Q. "Yes, among others how can you put these rather primitive earth sculptures in the same class as those of Michelangelo? He was a genius, a master of several arts."

A. I'm glad you asked this question because it lies at the heart of our misunderstanding of the sophistication of Native American cultures. I will make two observations and a comment for you to consider so that you might answer this question yourself. First, in Brotherston's book *Image of the New World* he notes that Chief Red Cloud predicted an eclipse of the sun in 1846, to the utter amazement of the white community in New England. He apparently understood something about "heavenly movement" he was not supposed to know. Second, on Highway 12 near Sauk City, Wisconsin, a roadside historical marker erected in 1957 makes the following observation about Chief Blackhawk who in 1832 led the Sauk Indians back to their ancestral lands in Illinois, thus starting the "Blackhawk War." Among the Americans who pursued and destroyed most of Blackhawk's people at the infamous Battle of Bad Axe were Abraham Lincoln and Jefferson Davis.[10] The historical marker reads as follows:

Battle of Wisconsin Heights

On the wooded heights southwest of here a force of about 1000 troops led by Gen. J.D. Henry and Col. Henry Dodge overtook Black Hawk and his band of Sauk and Foxes during a rainstorm in the late evening on July 21, 1832. With about 50 warriors Black Hawk fought a holding action on top of the hill to allow the rest of his people, including old men, women and children, to get across the Wisconsin River just beyond. The war ended 12 days later at the Battle of the Bad Axe on the Mississippi River where the Indians were all but wiped out. At Wisconsin Heights, as in no other phase of the war, Black Hawk displayed personal bravery and military skill of high order. Describing the holding action on the part of Black Hawk here, Jefferson Davis later wrote: "Had it been performed by White men, it would have been immortalized as one of the most splendid achievements in military history."

Finally, the comment has to do with the level of the communication in both constructions, Michelangelo and the builders of the mounds were both speaking in symbolic language using concepts such as night and day as the concrete anchor points of their metaphoric message. Later I will make a brief presentation of the relevance of this level of communication, but at this point it is enough to say that symbolic communication is a more integrated form and can communicate more information on more levels than is possible by using concrete "scientific" language.

Chapter VII

THE EQUINOX
Polarities Balanced

Within every man there is the reflection of a woman, and within every woman there is the reflection of a man. Within every man and woman there is also the reflection of an old man and an old woman, a little boy and a little girl.

— Hyemeyohsts Storm

What lies behind us and what lies before us are tiny matters compared to what lies within us.

— Ralph Waldo Emerson

Given this discussion of death, how can we understand the philosophy of life embedded and acted out in the lifestyle of these Native American Indians? Some clues lie in understanding the importance they put in the medicine wheel. The book that best explains the medicine wheel is called *Seven Arrows,* by H. Storm.[1] To understand the medicine wheel one has to understand how the Indians lived with the four directions of the compass to give them guidance and that there was meaning in each of the four directions. If the Native Americans felt that the wheel of the compass would help them to become oriented to the sacred directions during their journey on earth, why the need for medicine? And what was the illness?

The circle is a universal symbol of unity. The wheel of the compass and the wheel of time, circles that describe space and time, were deeply embedded in the everyday experience of Native Americans. The round of the seasons, the circle of the movement of the sun and moon, the round from birth, to adult, to old age, the circle of life. The wheel of the medicine wheel was a symbol that described the evolution of each person through the stages of life with the community of the tribe. The medicine of the medicine wheel was a psychological, spiritual process through which an individual came to identify himself with everything in the world around him. This ancient, simple model of spirituality is based on everyday observation. It is old but not a thing of the past. Consider it in the present. When a person sits in a circle with others meditating on an object in the center of the circle, the circle will become a reflector, a mirror through which the object in the center can be enhanced by comparing the description of the object by each person. Of course, each person will have a correct but partial experience and therefore description of the object. By interacting with the other persons and by respecting their views, a complete description of the object is possible. More, each person will come to know not just objects but himself through his interaction with each other person in the circle. Progressive identification of oneself with others and the things around one will then, in time, result in progressive opening to the levels of transcendent reality. And to complicate the process, one must "let go" of attachments to simpler conceptions of reality to embrace the higher. Finally, an attitude of non-attachment becomes embedded in experience and the world is experienced as an ever-turning kaleidoscope, as one beautiful "centered" pattern gives way to another beautiful pattern. The one dies to give birth to the next.

Confused? Let me say it this way. The tribe as a circle will bring whatever it addresses into focus, so everyone can "know" it, and by identifying with all of it, embrace more of the world and become more deeply identified with the tribe. Each person will come to know himself through his totem animal. He will come to know himself in a flower, in a river, and in a rock. As he moves through the four directions of the medicine wheel, the process of identification with objects, ideas, feelings, relationships, ideals, the community, the heavens, etc. grows. No position on the wheel is favored. Each has an important point of view when looking into the center of the circle. Understanding and experiencing the mystery at the center is only complete when one has moved through all positions around the circle. And the final stages of surrendering to the great mystery mean that one will identify but not attach, not hold onto one's experience. In the final stages, letting go of experience is the only way the, shall we say, *higher stages of experience* can in fact be approached. Dissolution of the vehicle of the spirit, that is the body, is required for the soul to move into the transcendent, spiritual realms after death. But listen to Nottwo.

A person is born to a position on the circle. In order to help orient to the perceptions of that position on the circle the person is given the help of a totem animal, a spirit helper. So that we might gain some understanding of this evolutionary process, we will start our journey around the medicine wheel in the south and proceed clockwise. In this way, we can gain a preliminary understanding of how they considered the process of psychological/spiritual change. We must remember that in reality the journey is not a continuous progression around the circle but is non-structured movement from one direction to any other, back and forth, until the journey is completed by an intuition and realization of The Mystery, conceived as existing in the center. The geometric form called a labyrinth, a mandala, that proceeds round and round, back and forth, ever inward, is a medieval geometric representation of the journey. The labyrinth on the floor of Chartres Cathedral in France is perhaps the most famous Christian description of this symbol of transcendence. But in order to understand the symbolism of the directions, listen to the following brief description of the meaning of the directions.

For the Plains Indians, south is the direction associated with birth, innocence, new growth, and youth. Because south is associated with beginnings, a clever teacher is needed to bring the novice along. Perhaps surprising, the coyote, a trickster, is often the totem animal associated with this direction.[2] The coyote is a teacher, a friend to students and teachers alike. Because some things are best learned through trickery, the coyote is allowed a wide range of moral and magical teaching tools. Carl Jung has completed the most scholarly explanation of the trickster cycle of the Ho-Chunk.[3] Wiley Coyote, the cartoon character, is a distant relative of this spirit helper. Green is the color associated with the process of learning, innocence, and new growth. Buds and flowers are symbols of this direction. South therefore has associated with it an animal spirit guide, the coyote, a principal concept, innocence and a color, green.

For us, childhood and time spent in school, college, or university would be time spent in the south.

As we move to the west, we enter the land of the setting sun. This is the direction where light turns to darkness. Black is the color associated with the west. We come to know the dark side of our nature in the west. It is associated with the concept of introspection. As we peer into the shadow of ourselves we discover a powerful instinctive realm that is identified as a black bear. Until we identify and accept the characteristics associated with darkness and animal power, we cannot move beyond this direction. Obviously, one must visit this direction many times on one's journey. In our psychologically oriented culture, time in therapy, or supervision or periods overwhelmed by addiction, would represent time spent in the west.

We move on to the north once we have gained a basic understanding of our conscious and unconscious nature. This takes time. The north is associated, therefore, with wisdom. And as the aging process causes our hair to turn white, and since cold winds from the north bring the snow, white is the color of the north. The Plains Indians identified the aged white buffalo as the animal spirit helper of this region. The buffalo has become wise because it has transcended the life-hunt-death-rebirth cycle in its temporal relationship with the Indians. Wisdom starts as we learn to share and give away what we have learned. Then we can give away our money, our knowledge, our love. Wisdom develops as we learn to give up our fears and desires. Time spent with grandchildren and in voluntary service is time spent in the north.

Finally, we move to the east. The wise know that the great mystery will not yield to the mind. It can be known but not explained. It can be perceived but not proven. So as the sun rises in the east, illuminating the manifest world, a person journeying to the eastern side of the medicine wheel will enter illumination. The color is the color of light, golden yellow. The animal effigy symbolic of the east is the eagle, a bird that can rise like the sun and gain a global view. From this heightened, almost visual perspective, the overall plan, not just of the people and their totems, but of all of one's relatives becomes clear. "All my relatives" comes to mean one's relationship with the rocks, plants, animals, and people. These relationships become manifest to the physical eye, then to the mind's eye, and finally to the eye of integration, or contemplation.

Now the process of the Medicine Wheel is one of movement around the circle; that's the wheel part of the Medicine Wheel. If identification and incorporation are the medicine, what is the sickness? The "sickness" that prevents this spiritual growth is loneliness.[4] When we cannot identify with the "things" around us, or feel separate from other persons, loneliness can overwhelm us. Whereas Buddha said that all life is suffering, and that fear and desire are the primary feelings that must be transcended to become enlightened, and whereas Freud identified repressed sexual feeling as the source of neurosis, preventing a sense of wellbeing, the Plains Indians believed that our experience of our individuality separated us from others and nature, and that the resulting sense of loneliness, or aloneness, was the dangerous state that needed to be overcome. The philosophical architecture of the medicine wheel and the spiritual ritual of the sweat lodge were part of the answer.

To repeat, the medicine of the wheel is the psychological process of identification. When one has an adventurous experience from one point of view on the wheel, identifying with all the objects, people, dynamics, etc. in that experience, loneliness will decrease as it integrates into the experience, rejoining that part of the person to the whole. Such experiences are the healing gifts, the balms, even the satoris that keep one on the path moving closer and closer to the center and a surrender to the mystery. Participating in the ecology movement, periods of withdrawal from the demands of economic and family life, and spontaneous holistic insights, are time spent in the east.

It is clear, then, that identification became important, that is being identified with all of one's relatives and all of one's environment was in fact the task that one should complete in one's lifetime by experiencing everything from all points on the compass. This process of identification is quite compatible with modern psychoanalytic theory, but it is even more akin to concepts of eastern religion. Buddhist and Hindu philosophies make more explicit the need to empty oneself of personal identification, i.e., ego, in order to move to the transpersonal plane and discover that "thou art that," meaning that you are everything. As one moves around the wheel, identifying with more and more of the experiential world, one's last journey would be with the eagle, toward heaven until, progressively leaving the eagle, one identifies with the *all*. This, in fact, was the great message of Nottwo. As a symbol of the birthplace of all "living" things, Nottwo the earth could only point to the ultimate realm symbolized, in an above/good, below/bad paradigm, the heavens, the place known by the eagle, an envoy who can connect the earth with the heavens. Nottwo made it clear that this was a time that the philosophy of the Medicine Wheel could take its proper place with the philosophies on the other great world religions. It is also the time that wisdom and illumination, the lessons of the north and east, are needed. The eagle's perspective is due. But the high ground to be gained here is much more than just height. When "The Eagle Has Landed" was broadcast from the moon to the earth, our species did gain new important perspectives. We saw an "earthrise" for instance. The valued perspective from the eagle is a global, integrated, detached vision of the interrelatedness of all creation, a clear view of the place of the individual person, in that set of relationships and the job for the lonely ego is to yoke (Yoga), to suture (Sutras), to re-ligate (religion) itself back into the seamless fabric of creation.

In the summer of 1991, as part of a four-day workshop organized by Chris and Dennis Merritt called "Spirit in the Land, Spirit in the Animals, Spirit in People," I was asked to explain aspects of the language of the mounds by examining the Turtle and Eagle Mounds on Observatory Hill, on the University of Wisconsin campus. So, on a cool, bright day, when the wind was still, we arrived at that point on Observatory Drive called the Scenic Outlook, high over Lake Mendota. Just beyond the University Observatory we looked to the right over the lake. It is a beautiful scene, one of the great vantage points from which to see the shoreline of Lake Mendota. Looking almost due north across the lake I could see the grounds of the Mendota Mental Health Institute and because I knew where to look, I could see the high ground containing the cluster of conical mounds that Dr. DeHarte had excavated. Turning around, we looked south up Observatory Hill. To the right of the Observatory near the zenith of the hill stands

OBSERVATORY HILL MADISON

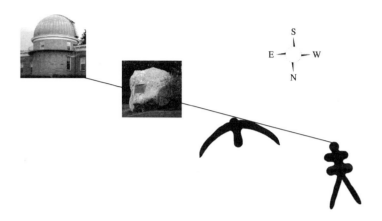

Figure 19. Observatory Hill rises to the east from the west. The progression then is from the Turtle Mound to the Eagle Mound, up past Chamberlain Rock to the summit and the current observatory.

Chamberlain Rock. It measures about twelve feet high, six feet across, and four feet deep. (See Figure 19.)

Thomas Chamberlain was a former professor of geology and president of the University. It had been his fortune to discover the origin of this rock, which he determined was a part of the Pre-Cambrian Shield in Canada that had migrated with the last ice age, called the Wisconsin, and had been deposited on the hill. A plaque commemorates his discovery and notes other dimensions of his tenure as professor and chair of the Department of Geology.

Our group assembled, we walked up the hill and decided to pause first at the rock. We read the plaque. I then asked everyone to walk around the rock and notice anything unusual about it. Aside from the plaque that was bolted into the rock, they did notice that the surface of the west side of the rock seemed to be flat. With our compasses and a simple string plumb line, we determined that this surface was in fact almost perfectly perpendicular in its north-south line. I had asked them to note the lines on the flat surface and then suggested that this was possibly a feature of the stone modified by man. I then asked them whether they had ever heard of gnomens? No one in the group had, so I explained that one type of gnomen was a rock light-shadow sundial that was used by native people to tell a specific time. I asked them to consider what change in the lighting might occur on the west surface of Chamberlain Rock on the equinox. After some discussion they were able to determine that the west face of the rock would in fact remain in the shadow until sometime around midday. They speculated that it would not take much time for the sun, just passed midday, to bring the west side of this rock into the light. I agreed. This rock appeared to be man-modified to mark midday on the equinox. The west face of the rock would remain in the shadow until the sun passed the mid-point of the day, when it would turn to light. The equinox was already a 24-hour day when there was equal light and dark, i.e. 12 hours of each. The surface of the rock would mark the halfway point during the day. I told them that our most recent validation of this observation, correcting for daylight saving time to "true noon" time, showed the rock was about 35 minutes off the correct midpoint. But I also showed them how the rock was slowly falling to the west due to erosion, and that if we corrected for this tiny three- or four-degree movement, the rock would come within minutes of midday for our latitude.

We then walked over to look at the two mounds immediately west of Chamberlain Rock. The first is an eagle. The State Historical Society has placed a plaque on it, calling it an eagle effigy. What the picture of the eagle shown on the marker does not show is that the wings of the eagle are not symmetrical. However, once we had reviewed the bird's position from all sides, it was clear that it was sculpted flying south up the hill and that its head is almost exactly at the crest of the top of the hill, as though it were peeking over, looking south. The long axis of its body was not, however, in a direct east-west line and I told them that if we had time we would come back and discuss that.

We then walked about fifty feet further west to the turtle mound. This mound also has a plaque on it placed by the Wisconsin State Historical Society. The plaque describes it as a "bifid" turtle. This is a very "artistic" turtle that has a well-defined head, two bulbous anterior limbs, a narrow body, then two bulbous posterior limbs, and then curiously, a bifid tail. The two parts of the split tail angled down and out for more than fifty feet in an easterly and westerly direction. The turtle appears to have crawled up the hill from the lake. The head of the turtle is also at the crest of the hill as though it could see over it, again looking south.

The slope of the hill west of the turtle has been markedly altered by University construction. Approximately thirty feet west, the land has been deeply excavated. The top of a two-story building lies below the turtle. The sidewalk that goes along the top of the ridge angles down so that people can walk down to the road that we had just come up from. There is no historical documentation, however, that there were any mounds further to the west of this position. Standing at the turtle and looking east we could look over the eagle, over Chamberlain Rock, and up to the high point of the hill where the University in its wisdom had placed the observatory, and we could even see farther on that the hill crested just on the other side of the observatory. There are remnants of some unknown mounds on that high point. I then directed their attention to the turtle and eagle mounds.

I pointed out that, at the dedication of Chamberlain Rock, the records show that a Ho-Chunk girl told a story about these two mounds. She said that the Eagle and Turtle Clans of the Ho-Chunk had formerly lived down on the Mississippi and that before historical time they decided to move up the Wisconsin and resettle in this area. She said that their oral tradition recorded that they had lived together in such harmony that they decided to construct these mounds as a way to celebrate that harmony.

The mounds were constructed on the east-west crest of the hill. They were part of a group of mounds built along the east-west axis, purposely placed to celebrate the harmony between the Eagle and Turtle clans. I told them that they were further connected to Spirit Rock in the University of Wisconsin Arboretum and to the principal burial mound on the grounds of the Mendota Mental Health Institute. I said that I would show them how the geometric construction was part of a pattern linking many mounds around Lake Mendota, and that it would help us to understand how the mound alignments could give meaning to the seven directions. A number of this group had read *Seven Arrows,* by H. Storm. They had made the connection that the seven arrows represented the seven directions—north, east, west, south, the direction up, the direction down, and the direction inside oneself. I said that I would try to put that very matrix in context for them, referring it to the medicine wheel.

First I noted that the two mounds were placed in an east-west line so that there is clearly meaning in their relationship to the east and to the west. (See Figure 19, again.) Things on an east-west line were thought of as in balance, symmetrical, or as the Indian woman said, "in harmony." I pointed out how the turtle mound, which was sculpted on the ground with its head rising up to the crest of the hill looking south and was about fifty feet west of the eagle mound on the east-west line, was farther down the hill than the eagle. In other words, in the rise of the hill on the east-west line, the turtle was lower, the eagle was higher, and Chamberlain Rock still higher, moving east on to the crest of the hill where the observatory was. I pointed out that the turtle was an animal that physically lived on the ground and in the water and that it was not by chance that they had placed this mound in an "inferior" position. I pointed out, in the reverse, that the eagle, whose head was sculpted to crest the hill looking south, as though both the eagle and the turtle had moved from the north to the crest of this hill so they could look over the hill, was higher up on the east-west line. I then pointed out that eagles, of course, spend their time flying and that their principal relationship with the earth involves rare contact with ground but considerable time in trees and in the air. The Indians, therefore, had placed these two effigies in their east-west relationship in the actual habitat relationship they have with the earth. I further pointed out that since we knew the history of these two mounds and knew that they celebrated the harmony shared by the two clans, that we could understand more clearly the syntax of an east-west alignment, i.e., an equinox alignment, by letting words like harmony, symmetry, balance, etc. describe or explain their relationship. And, in fact, we know from history that to be the case with these two mounds.

We had already talked about sacred geometry and the relationship of Phi so; they knew that there was a way to divide a straight line so that you could get the proportion, A is to B as B is to the sum of A+B. I said, therefore, that Professor Scherz' rigorous surveys had in fact determined that there was a Phi relationship

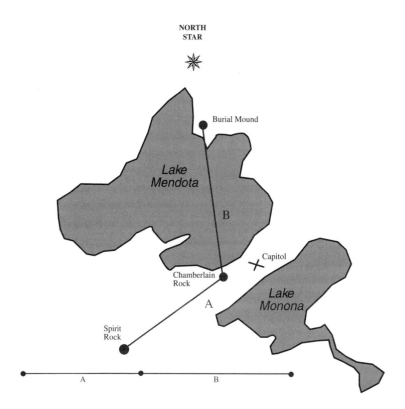

Figure 20. Phi Relationship between Spirit Rock in the University Arboretum, Chamberlain Rock on Observatory Hill, and the largest burial mound on the grounds of the Mendota Mental Health Institute, Madison.

between Spirit Rock south in the Arboretum and Chamberlain Rock as A and Chamberlain Rock and the Conical Mound north across the lake on the grounds of Mendota Mental Health Institute as B. (See Figure 20.) There was therefore a geometric relationship that gave meaning to these mounds in relationship to a sacred place in the arboretum in the south, that is Spirit Rock, where Native Americans go to this day to make offerings of tobacco, and a meaningful relationship with an important burial mound on the grounds of the Mendota Mental Health Institute to the north.[5] Spirit Rock, a sacred rock, is associated with the rituals of birth in the spring. The meaning of the direction south in the Medicine Wheel was birth, youth, life, and growth. These qualities are the classic features ascribed to the position south in the medicine wheel of the Plains Indians. The relationship with the burial mound north, across the lake, most obviously related to the other pole of life—death. While death is associated most strongly with the direction west, in this construction one could only speculate that the people buried on the grounds were wise, wisdom being the concept of the north. Since they were Eagle people, the eagle associated with the direction east, the meaning to the north was clearly complex integration of other directions, too.

I then pointed out that Chamberlin Rock played an integral part in this celebration of unity in duality because it appeared that the western face of that great stone had been modified in alignment in an east-west direction, making it possible to divide the light of day itself into two halves. Since the theme of these mounds was to celebrate the harmony experienced by two different clans, harmony that could even be thought of as unity, unity in duality, unity in difference, I told them that this could explain why they had put a second tail on the turtle. The exaggerated limbs on the turtle also give emphasis to the idea of twoness. I told them that when we got access to a blackboard I would explain the two key relationships that were hidden in the placement of the asymmetrical wings of the eagle.

Before I could do that, however, I wanted to explain how there was meaning in the directions, above and below. We reaffirmed as we looked at the two mounds that the turtle was in a lower position than the eagle to the east. We then noted that this represented a relationship in the above-below direction and that the turtle mound had been sculpted purposely below the eagle to represent its actual habitat in real life. The turtle lays its eggs in the ground, its young are born to the surface, it then moves on the land to the water. It also spends significant amounts of time below the surface of the water. By comparison, the eagle lays its eggs in a nest in a tree, its young are born to the surface of the air. Then, as they learn to fly, they also make contact with the ground. They spend most of their time soaring above the ground. The turtle represents the base upon which the earth rests and in fact several in the group knew that Native Americans called the North American landmass Turtle Island. Others made the association that in Hindu philosophy the turtle is the animal swimming through the ether upon which stand four elephants which hold up the landmass. Similarly, the eagle is symbolic of our contact with the heavens. Eagles soar. Some in the group remembered that the eagle was the usual animal symbol placed in the east because that is where the sun rises as it goes to the zenith.

Next, I pointed out that a turtle and an eagle could live in harmony in the same habitat because they were not actually in "competition" with each other. They forged for different food, their relationship with the land, the food source, nesting habits, etc. were in the same place but in a non-competitive manner. And therefore there could be a sense of celebration between the Eagle Clan and the Turtle Clan because in imitating and fully identifying with their animal totems they would not be in conflict with each other because they would be looking at different parts of the environment to sustain them. We had, therefore, in the directions of the compass and the directions up and down, accounted for purposeful meaning in the construction of these mounds.

Finally, I addressed the seventh direction. What could these mounds say about the inside of a person? For Native Americans "God" was a great spirit that had no form. The Great Spirit could be symbolically observed in the mist or in the sacred smoke of the pipe, a form so mysterious that it would hold for only a short time and then disappear into everything. They did not concretize the form of their god. In order to validate everyone's experience of the great mystery the people could describe their god as the Great Spirit. While they had rather frequent territorial wars, they rarely had religious wars because they held a respect for the ultimate religious experience in everyone and knew that it could not be described but only pointed to, more like Buddhism, than the concretized symbols of the Monotheistic religions. It is true that they had visions, but visions usually carried a message about the journey, not about the ultimate. And while many Indian nations developed a sophisticated architecture of the afterlife as a happy hunting grounds, none was expected to believe in the description as a fact. There were no dogmas, just life experience with all the sacred things of the Great Spirit. Consequently, these mounds could speak of interiorizing harmony or love as the "meaning" in the seventh direction.

My last interpretation to the group focused on the single word, *harmony*. When one first looks at the world, it appears to consist of opposing forces, like good and evil, up and down, hot and cold, east and west. This dialectical appearance in the west has left God at eternal odds with the devil, with all the usual problems. If God is everywhere, S/He must also be in hell. Or if God is everything, S/He must also be the devil, etc. But for those familiar with the philosophy of the Medicine Wheel these "problems" disappear. For instance, it is true when sitting in a circle that those on the other side of the circle will see an object between them from the "opposite side." But since everyone is expected to make a complete round of the wheel, everyone knows that in time they will experience for themselves that which seemed contrary to their original perception. This will allow the original view to be reality tested and the polarity, the opposite, to be transcended. Western philosophers have grappled with these oppositions but with linear logic. Theologians, too, are stuck in the belief that God, all good, should therefore be forever separated from evil, all bad. Only the mystical tradition has been able to reconcile these opposites. Sometimes we have to settle for this summation: "For God all things are good, but for wo/man things appear good and bad."

Then I pointed out to them what I had learned from Nottwo about this apparent conflict. When one comes to understand that we are related to everything, that our relatives are every aspect of the phenomenal world, from concrete rocks to mystical concepts, when all of that is integrated within us, the initial impressions that the world is presented in a contradictory process of apparent opposites hardens as though it were the final step on the way. But because the images are open to transcendence, the question comes down to a sense of two that disappear into one. I told them that I thought that the highest compliment that we could pay the people that constructed these two mounds was to acknowledge not just that they lived in harmony as people from different clans, but that they allowed each individual in each of the clans, in spite of differences, the opportunity to resolve the differences within their breasts in the seventh direction. Knowing that reality is a unity of opposites is the transcendent insight on any spiritual path. Resolving the "problems" of good and evil, self and other, friend and enemy, is finally to realize that you, you yourself, are both. You are good and evil. You are friend and enemy. You are you and the other. The philosophy of the Medicine Wheel is sophisticated enough to recognize that this insight can only result from a realization that the individual in identifying with everything, the friend, the enemy, empties one of an attachment to a "side," in a polarity. Such emptying allows both sides of the polarity to embrace, like the yin-yang of the Taoists. The symbol of these dancing opposites opens to the transcendent mystery of "God." Living out such a mystery is a gift. Trying to talk about the mystery reduces it to mystical concepts, to symbols, and in this case to two effigy mounds and a simple story.

We went silent for a while and then I continued. In coming to understand the relationship of specific mounds to moon and sun horizon events, to the North Star, and the way that some mounds were sculpted on the terrain to indicate movement, we were in reality coming to understand the syntax of the language system as earth writing. Furthermore, by identifying universal events in the geometric construction such as the encoding of the tilt of the earth, 23½ degrees, of marking the latitude, or incorporating Phi, the golden mean, added a sophistication to the constructions that would qualify their cultures as "high cultures" as measured by western anthropologists. To date, North American Indian nations have been considered "primitive" or low cultures because they did not develop mathematics and writing. In fact, the period of the construction of the effigy mounds represents a high point in cultural development at least equal to their Central American contemporaries. One day we will understand the writing of the mounds in greater detail so that finally we will, with the help of the Ho-Chunk and other nations, be able to read those "texts" that still exist.

Consider, then, how the young were taught this information. When a young Indian boy or girl was growing up, their first identification was with the family and the clan. Clan mounds would accent and emphasize the importance of their clan animal. Furthermore, members of a clan would live near the territory marked out by their clan animal. For instance, all hills more than nine hundred feet above sea level in the Madison area had mounds built on top of them. It is very likely that the mound type on top of a hill would represent the principal location of the particular clan that lived there.

When an adolescent boy was about to go through puberty and become an adult, he entered into a special ritual or rite of passage called the vision quest. At the time of the vision quest he would take on not only a possible second identity, depending on the vision that he experienced, but he would take on the responsibilities of an adult. As part of taking on those responsibilities he would be told another level of meaning of the mounds. For instance, he would be told that the mounds had alignments to the cardinal directions, to the equinox, to the North Star. This information would help him in understanding the seasons, the rutting of animals, the time of planting in the spring, etc.[6]

Finally, a small number of men and women would enter into the sacred lodges. The lodges were somewhat like the priesthood of conventional religions. They included the shaman and some tribal leaders.[7] The sacred information coded into the mounds required keys to read them. Part of the ceremony of entering into the lodge was that the lodge secrets were shared with the candidate. The eagle mound on Observatory Hill holds such secrets and they lie in the asymmetry of the wings of the eagle. Before I share these secrets, you should know that these observations were previously published by Professor Scherz in the *Journal of the Ancient Earthworks Society*, the annual publication of that non-profit group. These "insights" I believe have been shared with selected whites who have been identified by members of the Ho-Chunk lodges because they trust the information will be shared to promote preservation of the mounds. It is in the service of such preservation that I share them now.

First, look carefully at this eagle. If you check its orientation to the cardinal directions with a simple compass, you can see that the body of the eagle is not flying in a north-south direction. It is flying slightly off north-south. Furthermore, it is clear that the wings are asymmetrical. While they are the same length, the angle to the body of the eagle formed by each wing is different. What we can make of this?

In order to understand the information coded in the mounds we would need a blackboard. Let me draw the eagle in an approximation to an east-west horizontal line and show roughly the asymmetry

of the eagle wings vis-a-vis the body so we can see the angular relationships. The key to liberating the information coded in this bird
is given by using a sixty-degree angle. If we take a sixty-degree
angle westward, off the easternmost wing, it does not reach all the
way to the body. But what it does do is form a line that would connect with the North Star. (See Figure 21.) So, a sixty-degree angle
from the east wing will give us an imaginary line with the North
Star. We then take a sixty-degree angle eastward from the body and
then draw a line. The angle between the line with the North Star
and that line is 51.5 degrees, or the angle of phi, which is the golden
mean, the golden section, the angle of life. (See Figure 22 and the
Golden Shaded Angle). Finally, if we take one further sixty-degree
angle eastward, off the western wing, and then take an angle from
the North Star, we get an angle of 23½ degrees, which is the angle
that the earth is rotated on its axis as it rotates around the sun. (See
Figure 23 and the Black Shaded Angle). The angle 23½ degrees is
marked on all of our globes. The Tropic of Cancer and the Tropic
of Capricorn are 23½ degrees north and south of the equator, respec-
tively. The Arctic Circle is 23½ degrees south of the North Pole and
the Antarctic Circle is 23½ degrees north of the south pole. These
23½ degree markings on our globes are important sun markers
because they mark the movement of the sun from the equator in its
maximum swings throughout the solar year. If you are above the
Arctic Circle, you are in the land of the midnight sun during the
summer and during the winter you have complete darkness. The
reverse happens at the opposite pole.

Consider then that we have on one side of an imaginary line to
the North Star an angle which correctly identifies the tilt of the
earth's axis and on the other side an angle that is symbolic of
the golden mean, golden section, or what is sometimes called the
angle of life. This is the equivalent to saying on the one hand that
they were aware of the relationship of the earth with the sun and
heavens, and on the other that they were aware of the primary life
process involved throughout nature. We have one angle symbolic
of a heavenly connection and another symbolic of the life connection on earth, wed together on the axis mundi, symbolically
connecting the earth with the North Star, the heavens. This
construction was clearly purposeful. It was coded into this eagle to

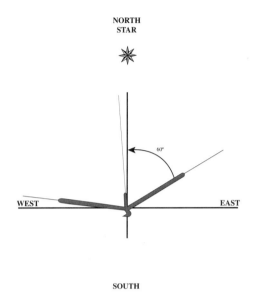

Figure 21. A 60-degree angle from the east wing gives an alignment to the North Star.

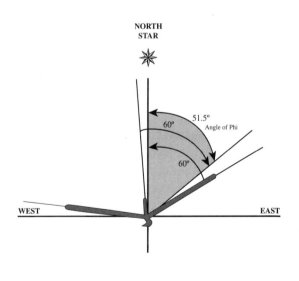

Figure 22. A 60-degree angle from the body toward the east wing gives an angle of 51.5 degrees with the North Star alignment.

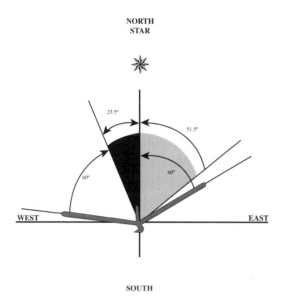

NORTH
STAR

WEST

EAST

SOUTH

Figure 23. A 60-degree angle from the west wing toward the body gives an angle of 23.5 degrees with the North Star alignment.

further embellish the critical ideas that are at the center of their sacred geometry. It is not just that the Turtle and the Eagle clans lived in harmony together, but that heaven and earth, and earth and life, can exist in harmony.

Just as Chamberlin Rock became a sundial to mark the mid-point of daylight on the equinox, the information coded into the wings and body of the bird is a further integration of two symbolic ideas in one mound. This leads us finally to the interpretation of the exaggerated twoness in the turtle. Remember, this turtle was called, by members of the Wisconsin State Historical Society in 1910, a "bifid" turtle. Its front limbs and back limbs were clearly pronounced, emphasizing their twoness. The fact that the turtle, however, was given two tails is also unique. When we consider that tails were symbolic of status, so that an effigy with an embellished tail had rank in the clan, then giving this turtle two tails gives added emphasis to the integration of two in one. One might even say in this day of left-right brain thinking, that the linear information coded in the eagle was left-brain linear thinking and that the information contained in the artistic bifid turtle was from the right brain, representing holistic, conceptual, symbolic thinking. As the earth's connection with the heaven (23½ degrees) can fit harmoniously into the earth connection (51½ degrees) with living processes, so "human" logical thinking can be integrated harmoniously with symbolic thinking, the eagle yielding linear logical information, the bifid turtle yielding conceptual symbolic information.

Mounds, therefore, had a direct association for those up to puberty with their clan identity. After the clan member's vision quest and entering into adulthood, the alignment information would be shared. And finally, those entering into the secrets of the Lodge would be given the keys to understand a further level of information coded in to some mounds. In the case of the eagle, the key to access the sacred information lay in the use of sixty-degree angles which would yield two powerful symbolic relationships. Much like the plays of Shakespeare which contain information for the peasant, for the merchant class and for the "intellectuals," mounds contain different levels of information, depending on one's position in life. Becoming aware of each of the levels of information has been a sacred journey that has slowly yielded its fruit through the intuition and dedication of investigators such as Jim Scherz, through the guiding and counseling of some whites by the Ho-Chunk and other tribes, and by what might be called direct intuition by those who have discovered the natural person in themselves and have lifted the veil from their own consciousness. They have reconnected with the roots of the earth and the earth's wisdom that is available to one as one would, in Native American philosophy, move around the medicine wheel.

Chapter VIII

THE GREAT EAGLE
The Return of the Executive

M*any situations can be clarified by the passing of time.*

— Theodore Isaac Robin

Nothing worse could happen to one than to be completely understood.

— Carl Jung

The car sped on the interstate up toward Wisconsin Dells. I had been asked by Larry Johns, an Oneida Indian, to make a presentation to elders of the Ho-Chunk and members of the Great Lakes Intertribal Council on the mounds at Mendota. I had my survey maps and slides. Furthermore, we had made a recent exciting addition to our understanding of the mounds in the eastern cluster and I was going to be sharing this information with this prestigious group for the first time. I couldn't help wondering how my presentation would be received. Furthermore, I was apprehensive because this is Native American history and not mine. I had gone through a long personal process of letting go of the desire to profit from my relationship with Nottwo and the insights about the mounds. I had had help from friends like Jim Scherz. Long ago in my presentations in the schools, I had begun with the caveat that the information that I was about to share would one day be taught by the Native Americans themselves. I was honored to be able to share it on their behalf because the information could help preserve mounds. By preserving and studying the mounds, we offered Native Americans and American society at large the greatest chance that the magnificent construction of the "mounds builders" would finally be appreciated.

We arrived at our destination and were met by a number of Ho-Chunk. They were quick to set up the slide projector and I began my presentation by pointing out the clusters of mounds and the alignments. I showed the diagrams of the burial that Dr. DeHarte had left. I pointed out how the four-legged deer was walking on the east-west line and went through the liturgy of the four-day journey to Earthmaker. I then pointed out how the panther mound, in my understanding, was often a symbol of a patron or guardian. It had been sculpted on a rise in the hill behind the eagles to give any traveler on the lakes or on the "old Indian trail" notice that this was a sacred ground. I also described what I called the outdoor cathedral up near the cluster of mounds, and then I came to the final handout.

Several years earlier we had discovered that a cartographer named Lewis had surveyed more than thirty thousand mounds in the Midwest in the late 1800s, principally in Wisconsin, Minnesota, Iowa, and Illinois, and that his survey maps were stored in the Historical Society of Minnesota.[1] After contacting officials there and finding little cooperation, help from our attorney general's office resulted in our obtaining copies of the Lewis surveys. While there were errors in some of the surveys, Scherz was impressed with the quality of Lewis' work. What was most exciting to me was that Lewis had surveyed our mounds, including the destroyed eastern cluster. By comparing Lewis' surveys with the modern survey of the extant mounds on the grounds, we were able to relocate the mounds in the eastern cluster, along Woodward Drive, and "put them back" in their original positions. (See Figures 24 and 25.). In this process, without being too critical, we were able to note some of the limits of Peet's field work.

I pointed out, therefore, that on the eastern edge of the eastern cluster there was a large conical mound that had two linear mounds converging to a spot just to the west of it. Then, moving west, there were three foxes, two with tails, one without a tail. The foxes were walking east toward the conical mound. Farther west, and flying away from the foxes, were three thunderbirds with an eagle to the north of the westernmost thunderbird. There were three thunderbirds flying west and three foxes walking east. Since I had already made the association between the three people buried in the prominent conical mound on the far western cluster with the three eagle effigies in the central cluster, i.e., two adults and a child, what amazed me in looking at the three thunderbirds was that there were clearly "two big ones and a little one." When I carefully examined the foxes there was no doubt that there were two with tails and one without a tail. The foxes were walking east, the thunderbirds were flying west. They were back-to-back in this construction.

Knowing that there was an east-west alignment from the principal conical mound through the wingtips of the eagles, and knowing that things on an equinox line are equal—or as the Indian girl said on Observatory Hill, are in harmony—and in making the association that we were dealing with threes—three buried people (two adults and a child) three eagles (two big and a little)—I could now add three thunderbirds (two big and a little) and three foxes (two with tails and one without a tail). I felt absolutely confident that the Fox Clan, as part of living in harmony with the Eagles, had built a parallel construction and that we could predict that the conical mound would lie on the east-west line with the principal burial of the Eagle Clan. In fact, when Scherz integrated Lewis' survey into the master survey, the east-west line that started with the eagle burial went right through the principal conical mound associated with the foxes. My prediction was validated.

At the same time I asked Scherz to measure the angle created by the two prominent linear mounds that were below and to the west of the large conical mound. Sure enough, when the lines of both mounds were extended until they met just west of the conical mound, they made an angle of 48 degrees. Given the measurements at the time Lewis did his work, that was a close enough approximation to 51.5 degrees to fit the sense of not only a harmonious construction, but a "parallel" construction, remembering that 51.5 degrees was represented in the angle of the two largest boundary linear mounds in the west. The following speculation was a small step. Could it be that the Eagle and the Fox clans had also lived in harmony and had decided to build a parallel burial construction? Having predicted that the conical mound would be on the equinox

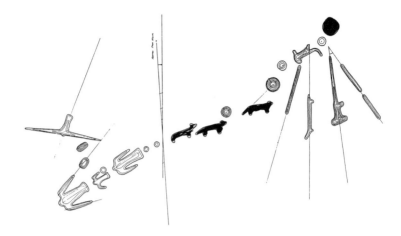

Figure 24. The Lewis Survey Map obtained from the Minnesota State Historical Society is much more detailed than Reverend Peet's map. In particular, Lewis shows two foxes with tails and one fox without a tail. Further, the middle thunderbird is clearly smaller than the other two. Finally, his map shows one Eagle Effigy Mound north of the thunderbirds, not two thunderbirds. This clarification makes the interpretation of "threes" quite plausible.

line, I made a further prediction which carbon dating could confirm. The Eagles were buried first, on the preferred high ground near the lake, as members of one of the upper region clans. (See appendix A.) Then the foxes were buried to the east. The thunderbirds, three in number and in the same ratio of two adults, one child, were sculpted flying away from the foxes because they are clans from different regions. Saying it another way, the thunderbirds and eagles are both clans from the upper region and therefore they fly the same way, or go in the same direction, opposite to but not against the foxes. At the same time it may also be that the thunderbirds, the most powerful clan, were incorporated into the construction to ensure that the eagles and the foxes remained in balance as though they had "approved" the plan. The eagles placement above the thunderbirds also supports the notion that the two clans from the upper

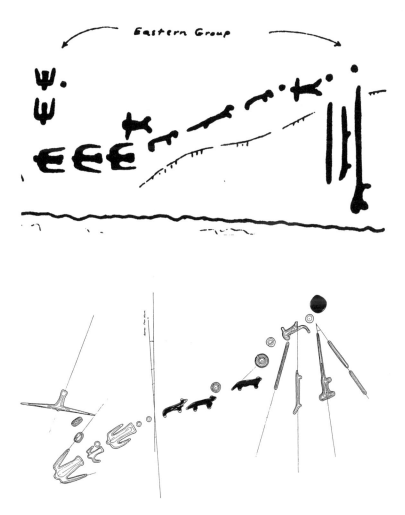

Figure 25. A comparison between the freehand drawing of
Reverend Peet and the survey of Lewis shows that the middle
thunderbird is smaller than its companions and that the bird
north of the most northerly thunderbird is in fact an eagle.
Both show three foxes, two with tails and one without a tail.

region are more closely connected. And as if to embellish the notion
that connecting two clans from different regions (the Eagles and the
Foxes) was an important event in need of respect and even protection, they placed a second panther mound below the easternmost

eagle, which could also ensure that there would be no outside disturbance between the clans.

After reviewing the foxes again, and noting that they were three in number but two with tails and one without, I concluded that the tailless fox must have represented a child. Since the burial on the high ground contained three people, two adults and a child, and the eagle effigies, the thunderbirds, and the foxes were also in that ratio, it did not seem illogical to draw that conclusion. This was made easier knowing that the mounds builders were infatuated with tails and loved to embellish them. Knowing that tails were a sign of status and position, not having a tail would indicate a child that had not gone through puberty, or more specifically had not gone through the rite of passage into adulthood. In this observation I suggested that we could identify another aspect of the syntax of the language.

I finally suggested that these foxes, two adults and a child, were representations of three people of the Fox Clan that would have been buried in the conical mound on the equinox line. I speculated that if we ever got the documentation of either the excavation of that mound or any reference that a farmer might have who had destroyed the mound, that we would find that three people had been buried in it, two adults and a child, and that they in fact would be buried facing east to finish the parallel and symmetrical construction. (But I hoped that they themselves would know who the Fox and Eagle people were and that they would tell me, but I held my questions.)

When I completed my presentation, I was pleased. I could see from the interest and soft eye contact of the Ho-Chunk people in the audience that they appreciated these possibilities. In their Indian way they asked quiet, modest questions. It was my feeling that I was not saying anything new, because I was quite sure that the oral history of this particular mound cluster was preserved within the lodges of the Ho-Chunk. As the afternoon wore on I finally asked whether they would tell me, before I died, the names of the Eagle Clan members who were buried on the grounds. They listened to my request respectfully. About a month later I was told indirectly that one of the elders knew the name of the person buried on Picnic Point, a piece of land that juts out into Lake Mendota, not far from Observatory Hill.

After the presentation, we noted that the work of the subcom-mittee on mounds preservation of the Dane County Parks Commission, which was chaired by Larry Johns, was about to be completed. The Ho-Chunk were pleased with the fact that a Native American had been chosen to head that project and it had resulted in the identification and documentation of hundreds of mounds that were not formerly known in Dane County. The cataloging and iden-tification of mounds had proceeded at a great pace. Furthermore, I was able to share with them the small role that I had played in making this presentation to Charles Chavla, a representative in the Wisconsin State Legislature. He was sympathetic to our mutual goals, including the preservation of Indian mounds. He signed on to a bill, passed by both houses, that precluded development within 25 feet of a mound, throughout the state. However, Governor Thompson, using his line-item veto, had scratched out the 2 and reduced the 25 feet to 5. Nevertheless, advocating for the mounds had obviously pleased the Ho-Chunk and they looked forward to the final decision that the Dane County Executive was about to make in regard to the final work of the subcommittee on mounds preservation.

It was a beautiful, sunny, Friday afternoon in late summer. The television crews had come onto the hospital grounds to the training center on Woodward Drive. Rick Phelps, the Dane County Execu-tive, had decided to hold a press conference in order to announce that the county had decided to implement a comprehensive plan to teach and preserve Native American History and their heritage, including their heritage as reflected in the earthen monuments called effigy mounds. He had decided to hold this press conference 25 feet from the world's largest eagle effigy mound, symbolic of the respect-ful space the county had granted the mounds.

With the cameras rolling and in front of a small but influential audience, he laid out his plan. It was formally described in the Sat-urday morning newspaper.[1] With the great eagle in the background as part of a comprehensive investment in preserving Native Amer-ican culture, he pointed out how there would be no construction within 25 feet of any mound in the county, the boundary defined as where the slope of the mound met the grade of the land. This news conference was the culmination of hard work by a number of people and it represented another important step in the raising of consciousness and appreciation of these Native American treasures.

That evening I had an unusual experience. Half asleep and half awake, a whoosh of sound went through my bedroom or my brain. Startled and yet reverently delighted, I appeared to be on the flyway of a magnificent bird. It swished through my bedroom, or through my mind, with great energy. As it made pass after pass, I was able to slowly adapt myself and be with it. As I did that an image of a golden eagle appeared. This bird was radiant. It smiled and flew on. No words were exchanged but I knew that the executive function of the eagle had been aroused and that the spirit of the chief of the Eagle Clan who was buried was now once again prepared to take his place in the living consciousness of Native Americans and whites. The spirits in the mounds had grown cold, but this attention had revived them. The eagle was awake and about to take off.

In the following days, because of the publicity in the newspaper, a number of people showed interest in having tours of the mounds on the institute grounds. I was able to conduct tours for many groups in twos and threes, and for some groups of up to fifteen. The greater the contact we had with the mounds the more the subtly of the construction became apparent. The syntax of the communication system became more beautifully unraveled and clearer to me. I could understand what we had been told, that the mounds were alive and that they told stories. Further, it was now clear to me that we had good examples in this protected collection of mounds of how the mounds could tell a story. We had a turtle that was pointing down a hill indicating its projected meaning as below its current station, down below the hill to the lake and then below the surface of the earth. Further, it had a meaningful alignment with the moon. We had a deer lying on the ground. By letting the deer stand up and walk, it connected meaningfully with an equinox sunrise, a specific point in time that occurs twice a year. We had birds, their projected meanings in the sky. The executive eagle and the smaller one, flying in parallel, were oriented to the North Star, to the zenith of the night sky connecting with the liturgy, which described the fourth door to be the zenith of the sun. The orientation of the executive eagle with the North Star was tantamount to saying, "We knew our relationship to that sacred spot in the sky."

The way in which the panther mound was laid out on a prominent hill that could be seen above the eagles showed it to be a
guardian, much as lions have been the guardians of portals throughout the ancient Mediterranean world. Here we had another cat that
was serving in the same protective guardian function purposely
sculpted on the only prominent rise, to call attention to the fact that
this is sacred ground. On and on the implications, like the way the
equinox was used to connect two large conical burial mounds in
the same line. Mounds were sculpted to tell stories, like the silent
statues in the Medici Chapel. Knowing the context of the placement
of these silent forms would allow one to tell the whole story, not
just the visible story of death, but the invisible story of the
conceptual mind and desire of souls to find unity with their maker.
Understanding the level of the communication is part of the transcultural adaptation required to understand their sophistication. Just
as most visitors and tourists miss the implicit communication in
the Medici Chapel, early explorers and later investigators missed
the importance of mounds. Even when told that the mounds tell
stories, like chapters in your books, they still didn't get it.

In order that we may more fully understand the levels of
communication of the mounds language, consider this simple order-
ing of communicative experience described by Masters and
Houston.[3] The first, most simple, and most direct level of communication is about "things" we perceive with our senses—for
instance a rock, a tree, a stream. They called this the sensory level.
The second level is to combine present sensations with those of the
past with the implicit comparison that arises. This sunset reminds
me of the first sunset I shared with my wife. Remembering and comparing enriches the present. They called this the recollective-analytic
level of communicative experience.

After a while, as our minds try to make sense out of more and
more life experience, some of us come to see that individual experiences, say of a rose, can grow to encompass all experiences of
roses. The form of one rose expands and connects with the form of
all roses, a "metaform" or using the Latin, a metaphor. That one
form can act or stand for other forms allows metaphors and symbols to communicate more levels of experience. Symbolic

communication is a more fully integrated level of communication. They called this the symbolic level of communicative experience.

Finally, for a select few individuals, a final integrated order of experience can be experienced once, perhaps twice in one lifetime. This transient experience, called *satori* by Buddhists, and *mystical union with God* by Christians, was called simply the *transcendent level of communication* by Masters and Houston. Transcendent experiences are also called ineffable because they are beyond words; words cannot express them. Poets try to communicate such experiences, but fail. So while one cannot communicate the experience in words, one can point to the experience. One can point the way. The Buddha didn't teach "Buddhism" but the way to Buddhism, that is enlightenment. So mounds align, that is point, to something else.

Using this system, mounds communicate directly on the first three levels. An eagle mound represents an eagle (level one). An eagle can also represent all eagles, the Eagle Clan, and their history as a clan (level two). The eagle can also represent a bird placed in the east of a philosophical system called the medicine wheel and symbolize the illumination of the rising sun (level three). Finally, in rare situations, particular eagles can hold in themselves, in the way they were constructed, symbolic ideas that can point the way to something beyond themselves, as the eagle on Observatory Hill does, (level four).[4]

The most powerful level of constant communication of key mounds in any mounds construction is on the symbolic level. Since most Euro-Americans are just now coming to understand and to operate on the level of metaphor and symbol, largely through their experience of movies, is it any wonder that the sophistication of these sign/symbols was not discovered as Euro-Americans moved west? (This is not to forget all the other powerful factors that underpin the American Holocaust[5] from manifest destiny to Christian proselytization.)[6] For us, though, understanding that the mounds were more than dirt sculptures can be a big step to reevaluating our conception of these "primitives." If we change our attitude toward their approach to life on this landmass, their role in American culture in the 21st century could have a positive impact.

Beyond understanding the different levels of communication, as I became more acquainted with the mounds I came to understand them to be living statements. They are alive in their movement, as the turtle goes down the hill, as the deer walks, and as the eagle flies. Right on the grounds of the Mendota Mental Health Institute, we have three beautiful examples of what the Elder who spoke with Dr. DeHarte must have meant when he said that the mounds were alive. What has happened over time is that the living energy that people bring during live ceremonies keeps the earthen symbol alive. The Ho-Chunk have lost control over many mound clusters. Of course, many of the mounds have been destroyed, but there are places in Wisconsin where they have not lost control of the mounds, neither have they stopped having ceremonies. What has been shared with some members of Ancient Earthworks Society is the effect that the living ceremony has on the mounds. Drummers are placed on key mounds. They drum up the energy of the mound and the people then dance with some of the mounds to form even more interesting patterns. The form of the earth plus the form that the people make at an organic and inorganic integrated image has even more impact than simply looking at the mounds by themselves.

There is no doubt that the mounds had a significant impact on the Native Americans, especially those who were able to read all the information in them. But even those who weren't able to relate to the mounds in a sophisticated way, could relate to them as we relate unconsciously to stop signs, to signs on the highway that will identify a rest area, to signs warning of a deer crossing. The information carried in mounds was not just specifically about birth and death, but in their cosmology, about all the events that shaped their lives. The mounds constituted a complete vocabulary to help them communicate about all aspects of their lives.

Chapter IX

THE GHOST EAGLE
The Spirit Returns

ccording to the teachers, there is only one thing that all people possess equally. This is their loneliness.

— Hyemeyohsts Storm

Everyone once, once only. Just once and no more. And we also once. Never again. But this having been once, although only once, to have been of the earth, seems irrevocable.

— Rainer Maria Rilke

It was a beautiful, crisp fall afternoon. We were celebrating the fall equinox. A number of us had driven out to a farm near Watertown, Wisconsin, where some friends had constructed a sweat lodge. Fred Gustafson, an ordained Lutheran minister and a Jungian analyst trained in Zurich, had completed the four summers of the sundance on the Sioux Reservation, at Rosebud in South Dakota, and in this process had became skillful at leading sweats. Dennis Merritt and I had driven out from Madison and were looking forward to seeing people whom we had not seen for some time. When we arrived at Kathy and Tony's, the fire was already burning high. We went through the usual greetings and met a group that would swell to eighteen. We exchanged some of the exciting news that had transpired since the last sweat in which I had participated, at the previous summer solstice.

After the friendly greetings, we sat around on the log benches catching up on the news. I was able to share that with the progress of legalized gambling at the Ho-Chunk Casino in Wisconsin Dells, the Ho-Chunk had been able to purchase a parcel of land on the Wisconsin River, about 640 acres in Eagle Township. This area was noted for a number of conical mounds. Even though there were apparently no longer Ho-Chunk Eagle Clan members in Wisconsin, the fact that they had been able to purchase this piece of land which used to have more than fifty eagle effigy mounds, was truly exciting. Even more important, Professor Scherz had had an opportunity to survey the mounds cluster there, so I passed on some of his preliminary findings. There was a long line of about thirty conical mounds that dotted the shoreline of the Wisconsin River. Farther inland from this long row there had been a number of eagles that at first glance showed no particular pattern or formation. In fact, as we spent more time looking for patterns, we were struck by the idea that the composition appeared to be an "assembly" of eagle effigies, the majority of which were pointed in the direction of the southwestward flow of the Wisconsin. Others had their wings in different positions, i.e., they were not in the general T-shape of an eagle in flight but appeared to be landing or taking off, while others were flying east. The overall gestalt seemed to indicate that this was an assembly area, perhaps the last one, that the Eagle Clan had used before their migration down the Wisconsin. Vague stories suggested they had held ceremonies for perhaps as long as four weeks saying goodbye to their buried ancestors.

I was also able to report that it appeared that a very large eagle, larger than the eagle on the grounds of Mendota by perhaps another five hundred feet, appeared to be resting in the terrain of what was now a farm. This eagle, now called the Ghost Eagle, was fully on the land that the Ho-Chunk had purchased. We cheered for the greed of American society that they could so generously contribute to the Ho-Chunk at the casino, which provided the principal funding source for the start of the buy back of this sacred land of the Eagle Clan. Comparisons were made to the early resettlement of Palestine by the Jews, who literally bought back large tracts of their ancestral lands before being granted a homeland by the United Nations in 1947. We hoped that the Ho-Chunk Casino and others in Wisconsin would continue to thrive so that the Indians would be able to reclaim additional important pieces of land.

Dennis Merrit, the president of the Ancient Earthworks Society, had talked with Professor Scherz and other members about the possible existence of this eagle, now plowed flat. There were in fact some early drawings of the site and Professor Scherz was already assembling a team to go out and determine the exact site of the mound by examining soil samples, a technique that he had applied to map the boundaries of damaged mounds at Mendota. This mound was called the ghost eagle because of the faint image of the mound on the aerial survey. The mound appeared to have a wing span of perhaps 1,300 feet. Alignments, however, were not clear at this point. Professor Scherz had determined that other extant mounds on the hilltops nearby had the expected alignments to solstice and equinox points. It made it very possible to think that the eagles that were assembled inland from the burials were in fact designed to commemorate their last offerings in Wisconsin.

Members of our particular sweat lodge were interested in all aspects of Indian lore and it was not surprising that they had many questions. I reminded the group that, just two years earlier, Dane County Executive Rick Phelps had held a press conference from the grand eagle on the grounds at the Mendota Mental Health Institute, and that this event was identified as the re-energizing of the executive function of the Great Eagle Clan chief who was buried on that prominent point. We seemed to be participating in a slow but sure reactivation of the power and energy of these mounds. Someone commented that the process, slow but sure, was the way of the turtle. Was Nottwo, in wisdom, guiding the return of the eagles?

The sun began to set while we sat around the fire which was heating the rocks for the sweat. We were sharing stories. When it was my turn I decided to respond to a question someone had asked me at the last sweat. They wanted to know how the mounds involved a sense of movement. So I reminded the group of the turtle, the deer, and the eagle, and how we could read meaning into their projected movement by knowing "where they were going," i.e., the turtle to the moon, the deer to an equinox sunrise, and the eagle to the North Star. I then retold the Frank slide story.[1] Somehow, the Indians knew that if all the animals moved off Turtle Mountain something was up. The movement of the animals had meaning. They knew how to read the meaning of the movement, and it saved their lives. When Turtle

Mountain crashed down into the valley, killing the residents of the town of Frank, the Indians could only watch in horror. The mountain crashed into the valley, burying the town under seventy feet of rubble. It crossed the town and buried the Trans-Canada Highway.

I told them I knew another story about a turtle crossing a road.[2] Middleton, Wisconsin, is a city of about 15,000, contiguous with Madison. In 1987, an area developer decided to build a middle-class suburb on the Madison side of the common border. The Madison authorities issued a building permit. A county zoning code specified that the developer needed access to Middleton Street, in Middleton, for the service of emergency vehicles (fire, ambulance, etc.). Confident that Middleton authorities would grant him access, the developer began construction before researching his legal obligations to that city.

The area to be developed was also adjacent to an environmentally sensitive area called Strykers Pond. Middleton Street formed one boundary of the pond. Were Madison residents to be given access to Middleton on that street, a quiet neighborhood would be turned into a busy and potentially dangerous shortcut between the two cities, and the projected increase in traffic would present considerable danger to the animal and plant life at the pond. Concerned Middleton residents who lived adjacent to the pond arranged for a University of Wisconsin group to conduct a series of environmental impact studies. Linda Souma, who lived on Middleton Street, decided to ask the pond for a sign that would indicate that the pond itself wanted the road to remain closed.

When the Middleton residents first approached the Middleton City Council to solicit support to keep the road closed, only one council member offered support. The majority of the council were interested in maintaining a good relationship with the developer. Since the residents persisted in their request that the Middleton council oppose the opening of the road, a date was set for the council to decide whether they would put up funds to challenge the developer in court.

At about three o'clock in the afternoon of the day that the council was to vote on the issue, a painted turtle walked up from the pond, across the road and onto Linda's property, dug a hole, and laid eighteen eggs, covered the hole, and returned to the pond. Linda recorded most of the process with her home video camera. She and her husband edited the hour-long drama down to ninety seconds. The edited tape showing the turtles work was the last item presented at the council meeting. Partly influenced by the tape, the council voted 6-1 in favor of keeping the road closed. As a result the developer took the issue to court and continued construction. In the interim, the road remained closed. Two years later the Wisconsin State Supreme Court decided in favor of Middleton. The road would remain closed. The day the decision was made public in the newspaper, another turtle appeared on Linda's lawn. This was only the second time she was aware that a turtle had been on her land. I witnessed this turtle firsthand. Could the turtles have communicated any more directly?

So animals could herald future events as in the Frank Slide, they could also communicate in the present like the turtle from Strykers Pond. The animal effigies could therefore be understood in these contexts. They not only pointed to celestial bodies acting as real physical "envoys" from the heavens, they could also communicate some of our most sophisticated ideas, like phi.

By now, the fire was burning down, and since we had four new people who were going to sweat with us for the first time, Fred Gustafson introduced them to the structure and purpose of the sweat. As the stones were heating up he said that he had participated in a number of different types of sweats with various bands of the Sioux on the Rosebud Reservation, and that the sweat that he and his wife were about to lead was structured in four rounds. He described the sweat lodge, noting it resembled a turtle and pointing out that it was based on an east-west line. The fire pit was currently at the head of the turtle and the pit that the stones would be put in to as the heart of the turtle. After clarifying that the line between the fire pit and the center pit in the lodge was not to be broken, he described the four rounds of the sweat.

The first round consisted of singing praise to the seven directions. This song was sung in the Sioux language. Most of us had learned the songs and the new people were encouraged to sing along as best they could. Since there were refrains that were repeated, they were told that they would likely catch on to the sounds of the words by the time we sang to the seventh direction. First we sang to the four compass directions, invoking the grace of grandmother and grandfather, and then we sang to the earth, to the sky, and then to the space that is within us all. The second round was a prayer round. In that round, in the dark of the sweat, each of us could share whatever we wanted. We could petition for health, we could celebrate our bounty, we could confess sins, we could resolve to make amends. People could remain silent and pass. The round could take whatever form that anybody wanted. Fred also explained that the person to pray first would be the last into the lodge, and that we would progress, following the direction of the sun, i.e., in clockwise order, until it came to him. He would be the first person to enter the lodge and he would remain at the door.

The third round was the pipe round. Fred pointed out how two pipes would be used tonight, that they were both filled and would remain outside the lodge near the alter fire pit. He showed us how to hold the pipe, to take one or two puffs, point the bowl of the pipe in the four directions, make an inner prayer or acknowledgement, and then pass the pipe to the left. We would do that in silence until the pipes had passed around to him and then he would put them out. At that point a cup of water would be passed and we would be allowed to drink. In general, we would remain in silence while the water was passed. The sweat would then end with the fourth round.

The fourth round was a celebratory one in which a number of songs were sung. Some were sung in the Sioux language but they could be any song that anyone wanted to sing. Sometimes, good old '60s folk songs from "Michael Row the Boat Ashore" to "Blowin' in the Wind" were shared. It was a time simply to relax and hang loose. Several questions were asked about the origins of the sweats and what other forms sweats took. Before we entered into the sweat, Fred asked me to lead the group in the meditation that Nottwo the Turtle had shared with me. I felt honored to do this.

By this time the fire had died down, the rocks glowing orange-red. We were in our bathing suits and some of us were cloaked in a towel. Otherwise we were barefoot and open to the elements. We were standing around the fire, shoulder to shoulder, and were ready to enter the lodge. At Fred's request, I led the group in a preparatory meditation.

I asked everyone to close their eyes and center on their breath. After they took several breaths to relax their bodies, I walked them through a simple relaxation exercise, starting with their feet, their legs, their torso, their shoulders, their arms, their neck and their head. Once they were relaxed, I asked them to focus on their face. I asked them to imagine their own identity as they would look at themselves in the mirror. I asked them to try to remember the image of their face and to let themselves be that person, a person rested and prepared for the adventures of a new day. I asked them to try to distill, from their facial image, their own conception of themselves, and to hold that as constantly as they could in their mind's eye. I gave them several minutes to enter into the process of comfortably identifying with their persona, and then from their persona to the true sense of themselves incorporated as a visual image. I added that they should let this image encompass all of the self that they could identify with, and all of the self that they had difficulty identifying with. And in this way, using a general Jungian structure, I tried to have them invite their shadow into their persona, and in the melding of these two that they would come to some idea of their ego. This "image," their ego, would then be called by their first name. I encouraged them to say their first name quietly to themselves.

Then, in preparation for the journey that we were all to embark on, in the sweat, I asked them to let this sense of themselves start a journey within their own body and to let it travel from the locus in their head down through their neck and into their chest. I gave them several minutes to complete the journey and suggested they identify themselves as a hot coal that was slowly dissolving in ice and that they let this coal dissolve and drop slowly until it reached the middle of their chests and rested near their beating heart. I asked them then to let themselves pulsate with their heart, to feel their pulse, to feel the warmth of the blood of their heart as it nourished them and to let the blood of their heart nourish their concept of themselves. In that posture I asked them to let all the positive things that they liked about themselves pour into the blood stream. At the same time I asked them to let all of their negatives, the things that they didn't like or couldn't manage about themselves, the things that would be called the shadow, empty into their heart so that goodness pumped out of their heart as their shadow fed back into their heart to be renewed. After several minutes of holding themselves next to their pulsating heart I asked them to bring themselves back out, up through their neck, into their face, and then to take this a step farther and let themselves come out an opening in their head.

In this process they were to allow all the love that they had for themselves to join with the concept that they had of themselves so that their ego life, their thought life, and their soul life would be enriched with love. I asked them to recognize that, as their heart nourished them with every beat, the love that they had for themselves represented in their own heart could also enrich their relationships with family, friends, strangers, enemies, with all their relatives.

We then observed a period of about two minutes of silence in which each person found their own way back into their face and head and beyond. I then closed the prayer by saying that we had replicated what a turtle does when it brings its head into its shell. It brings its mind into its heart to be nourished, and when it brings its mind out, it brings its mind out with heart.

That said, we entered into the sweat lodge. That evening each round was powerful. We sang to the seven directions, we prayed for things beyond the telling, we entered into the intimacy of pipe smoke, that primary experience of birth, the inhaling of air, the inhaling of smoke, blowing it out as the cleverest symbol of the Great Spirit, the spirit of breath, the spirit of inspiration, the spirit that has transient form, a symbol beyond bread and wine, beyond the function of life that is prior to food, that is breath. And finally we sang with joy the song of the eagles, realizing that they were on the rise and that the Eagle Clan was in the process of being reborn to its native land in Wisconsin. Following the sweat as we were cleaning up and putting our clothes on, Fred noted that since the birth of the white buffalo in Janesville, the sweats had become more intense.

Epilogue

WHITE BUFFALO CALF WOMAN

M*any could forego heavy meals, a full wardrobe, a fine house, et cetera; it is the ego they cannot forego.*

— Mohandas Gandhi

Come, love! Sing on! Let me hear you sing this song-sing for joy and laugh, for I the creator am truly subject to all creatures.

— Mechtild of Magdeborg

On August 20, 1994, in Janesville, Wisconsin, the Heider family, ranchers who raised buffalo, had the privilege of birthing a white female buffalo calf.[1] Genetic studies have taught us that about one in ten million buffalo are born with a white hide. For Native Americans, especially those whose totem animal was the buffalo, a white buffalo was a sign from the Great Spirit that bountiful times had come.

As we noted in the presentation of the medicine wheel, the white buffalo is the totem animal of the North. The white buffalo, therefore, represents wisdom that leads to bounty. The white buffalo also represents opportunity that comes only in a special age. Thus, when the Heider family realized that they had the good fortune to have a white buffalo born on their land, they immediately shared the news with the Ho-Chunk. A great message then went out to all Native Americans that the Great Spirit had sent a miraculous sign. The newspapers noted that the birth of the white buffalo calf could be compared to the second coming of Christ. This rare event was truly astounding. Ho-Chunk and Indians from other nations have since made pilgrimages to the Heider farm to see the calf. These journeys honoring the calf continue to the present time. The magic, the awesome respect, the wonder, grace and optimism that they have experienced in seeing this calf can only be considered transformative. The presence of this calf which, in the lodges, would be referred to as White Buffalo Calf Woman, a well-known mythological figure symbolic of the bounty described above, can be only distantly appreciated by those not familiar with this tradition. With time and humble enthusiasm, those outside this tradition will be able to share the joy the calf has brought her peoples.

This story then ends by closing further observations on the Indian mounds and by noting that the Ho-Chunk, enriched with gambling money, have been able to start the process of purchasing sacred ancestral lands with the clear recognition that a bountiful time has begun for Native Americans. The birth of the white buffalo calf has heralded an unshakable optimism in the lodges that will become clear to other North Americans: that we will enter a new era of relationships in what the whites call the twenty-first century.

And, it is said that members of the Eagle Clan have been seen walking their ancestral lands, here in Wisconsin.

Appendix A

THE BLACKHAWK MOUNDS
AND NEW BEGINNINGS

The Ho-Chunk (formerly the Winnebago) and other Indian nations who lived here before European contact, left as part of their cultural legacy burial and effigy mounds. The mounds were constructed from about 450 B.C. to 1500 A.D. and served many functions.[1] In general, the mounds were of two types. First, there were burial mounds which include both linear and conical forms. For thousands of years the Ho Chunk buried their dead in graves shaped in long lines, the linear mounds, or in "heaps of dirt" shaped like half a sphere, the conical mounds. The distribution of the burial mounds shown in Figure 26 defines part of the Ho-Chunk territory. Then around 500 A.D. (most authorities agree on this date) a cultural transformation occurred. They began constructing a second type of mound called effigy mounds. Effigy is French for *portrait*. The earth-sculpted forms of animals told some of the stories important to their way of life. Some consider the effigies an art form, and for others they are both a creative artful development and a form of earth writing, a kind of written language. A review of the distribution of the effigy mounds in Figure 27 shows that they are not as numerous as the conical mounds and that they were usually constructed near rivers or lakes. Figure 27 shows their distribution. You can see that the eastern banks of the Mississippi, Lake Winnebago, and Lake Koshkonong have mounds all along the shoreline

Lapham, Brown, Peet, Lewis, DeHarte, Stout and Radin[2] all described mounds and made attempts to interpret what they might mean as they consulted with Ho-Chunk and other tribal authorities. More recently the State Historical Society of Wisconsin[3] in

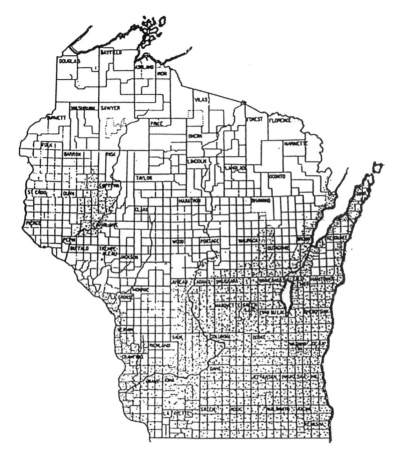

Figure 26. Map of Wisconsin showing distribution of circular mounds.

conjunction with Ho-Chunk elders and private groups, including the surveys of Scherz, have continued the tradition of identifying and protecting mounds and making further attempts to understand what the Ho-Chunk intended by their construction.

While many of the theories of the "meaning of the mounds" are well intentioned and interesting, most are contaminated by intrigue, fantasy, and just plain error. For instance, the mounds were not built by an ancient race, now extinct, called the Mounds Builders, as suggested in the *National Geographic Magazine*.[4] Nor were they

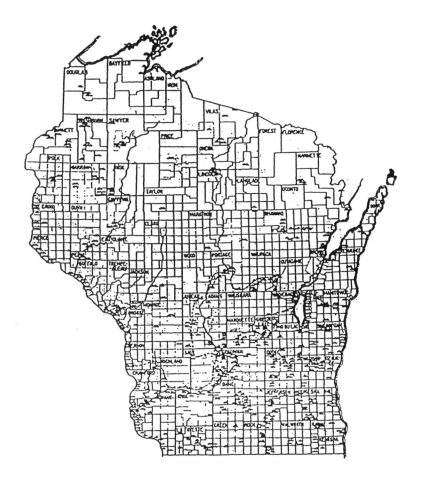

Figure 27. Map of Wisconsin showing distribution of effigy mounds.

constructed by the lost tribes of Israel. Our fascination with antiquity naturally tends towards grandiosity. The simple truth is that the mounds were constructed by the ancestors of the Ho-Chunk, Menominee, and other Indian nations. Furthermore, many of the mounds are not "ancient." Some were built within the living memory of elders interviewed by Radin between 1908 and 1913. But as I will suggest, the mounds did "tell stories" and there were different levels of information "coded," for lack of a better word, within them.

Until the Elders of the Ho-Chunk and other nations tell us what an individual mounds group means, we can but make the first approximations to that meaning in good faith. The thrust of this short essay then is to describe "the story" of twelve mounds now protected under the federal Historic Sites Act to illustrate how mounds can "tell a story." For intellectual honesty the reader should know the principles underlying my basic orientation to interpretive research. They are as follows:

1. Several Indian nations, all of whom were based largely in Wisconsin, buried their dead in linear and conical mounds for several thousand years.

2. Around 500 A.D. effigy mounds began to appear, and with them the nations, using alignments with the sun and moon solstices, and equinox, and intimate understanding of the ecological life style of each particular animal, created earth-sculpted effigy mounds to "document" facets of their cultural life.

3. The evolution of the story telling, in written mounds form, must await carbon dating of the various mounds clusters, especially the principle mounds (since mounds were later constructed on many sites) so that the development of the "grammar" can be better understood. By this I mean, when they first began using effigy mounds, they must have started with a simple plan and then developed greater sophistication by using effigies in combinations to tell a story.

4. The Ho-Chunk Nation consisted of twelve clans. (There may have been as many as sixteen or as few as eight or nine, depending on the historical period and the way the clans of the upper region [the birds] were counted.) The upper regions consisted of four clans, all birds—the thunderbirds, hawks, eagles and pigeons. The thunderbirds were the chiefs, the hawks were the warriors, the eagles were war "deities." The pigeons were extinct by the time the Europeans arrived and their specific function is not clearly known. The animals of the lower region consisted of the water spirits who were the "chiefs," the bears who were soldiers, and then the deer, elk, wolf, buffalo, snake, and fish.

5. Single effigy mounds were mainly clan markers of gardens, hunting posts, strategic positions, etc. When clans were in that particular area they usually camped by their clan mound.

6. Clusters of effigy mounds always seem to include a mound of one of the major clans, leading to my contention that the principle clans were responsible for constructing the mounds and that knowledge of these clans is necessary to know the exact meaning of any cluster.

7. Clusters of single clan mounds such as the ten Water Spirit "Panther" Mounds at the forks of the Manitowoc River, or the ten Marching Bears on the high ground on the west bank of the Mississippi, were clearly important as territorial markers for these clans. The Water Spirit Clan were guardians of the depths. They therefore guarded important areas, such as the forks of a river, but were also guardians placed in relationship to the river or water of any specific mounds cluster to ensure that the potentially evil spirits that lived under the waters would not harm that mounds cluster. In a similar way the Marching Bears of the lower region, who worked with the hawks of the upper region, were soldiers, and were clearly placed on the high ground on the west bank of the Mississippi for strategic reasons. There they had easy access to the Yellow River and could control traffic up and down the Mississippi or from the Wisconsin into the Mississippi.

8. Given that there were twelve clans, we can account for the fact that there were nearly one hundred different animal, bird, and fish effigies by suggesting that each of the non-clan effigies had a general and specific meaning. By this I mean that the major clans used the non-clan effigies to say things that were part of that animal's life cycle as that information would "fit" into the story. The way the goose is laid out in the construction below or the way the four-footed deer is laid out on the grounds at the Mendota Mental Health Institute are good examples of how non-clan effigies were incorporated into a construction with meaning.

9. In coming to understand or interpret a mounds cluster, the first step is to decide what the principle clan effigy is and assume

that that clan was responsible for the "story" and the actual construction, and that other effigies were chosen from the lexicon of animal effigies for the purpose of conveying information.

10. Even without knowing the specific meaning of a non-clan effigy, an interpreter can come to understand the general meaning of a non-clan effigy by understanding its life cycle and its other attributes. Until we get the help of the Ho-Chunk, we can make an approximation to the meaning of a mounds cluster. With this humble attitude, let us continue to examine the mounds at the Blackhawk Country Club.

As a bicentennial project the executive board of the Blackhawk Country Club in Shorewood Hills, Wisconsin, near Madison, asked L.J. Markwardt, the honorary club president, to take on the responsibility of identifying the boundaries of the mounds located on the golf course, so that they could be protected under the federal Historic Sites Act. Once this was accomplished, Markwardt wrote two short books that described the mounds and gave his interpretation of what the mounds might mean.[5, 6] One goal of this essay is to celebrate his contribution, along with the members of the Blackhawk Country Club, by offering further observations about the possible meanings of the mounds' complex.

Look at the figure outlining the mounds as described in the Historic Sites book. (See Figure 28.) One is immediately struck by the dominant mound, the goose. Its body and neck were measured at over 200 feet and its wing span 135 feet from tip to tip. The figure cannot show it, but since the mound is sculpted going uphill, it is clearly in flight. In front of it, but now destroyed, was a hawk mound. Over to the west there are three conical mounds and north of these are three linear mounds. Near the shoreline there is a panther mound and then over to the far northeast are three bear mounds. The total composition was twelve mounds (now eleven since the hawk was destroyed in 1920), including three conicals, three linears and six effigies.

Since some elders of the Ho-Chunk, now lost to history, told early Europeans that the mounds "tell stories like chapters in your books," there has been interest in understanding what those stories might have been. A single mound, however, usually did not tell a story as much as it represented a "property" marker. Radin, in his

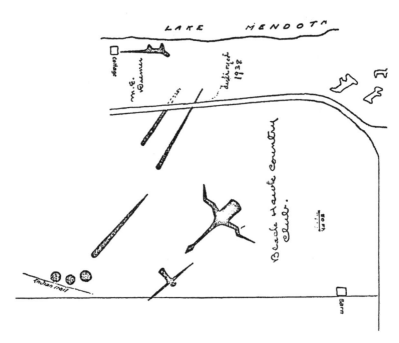

Figure 28. Schema of all 12 mounds protected under the Historic Sites Act at Blackhawk Country Club, Shorewood Hills, Wisconsin.

book *The Winnebago Tribe*, is quite clear on this point. When a particular clan entered an area they would usually camp near one of the effigy mounds. A single effigy might also mark a garden, a field of corn, a hunting post, or a strategic position. So single mounds were often nothing more than location markers that identified what clan had claimed the area. To reinforce this idea, images of clan animals similar to the effigy images have been found in bead patterns on clothing and painted on clan pottery. To date there have been no examples where beads or pottery appear to portray complex stories, as for example the pottery of the Greeks or Romans did.

Remember that the Ho-Chunk named their clans after animals. Most authorities record that there were twelve clans, divided into those that ruled the upper region, such as the Thunderbirds and the Eagles, and those that ruled the lower region, including the Bears and the Water-Spirits. However, there were three main clans, the Thunderbirds, the Bears and the Water-Spirits, when the Europeans arrived. According to most versions of their history, the Water-Spirits were originally the most powerful clan and controlled the other clans because they had their power from the depths, from the underworld. (Remember that there were no volcanoes in this region, so there were no volcanic gods, nor were there volcanic passages to the lower world. Water, including springs, were the main way the Water Spirit surfaced). Then they were overpowered by the Thunderbirds who became the ruling clan. The Water-Spirits, however, continued to influence the lower region and because they had been relegated to second place, so to speak, they were considered both "good" and "bad." They had power to do both and were thus considered as a sort of water monster. It was thus that in their effigy form they were usually represented as "panthers," often with the great long tails. (They were a sort of dragon with Hermes qualities, if we need a western comparison).

. Now look at the goose. The most hardened skeptic would have difficulty denying that it is flying to the southwest. The body and neck are in one long, straight line pointing in that direction. It we assume that they laid out the mound in a purposeful way, then letting the goose fly on its journey will result in an interesting destination. The goose is flying toward the place on the horizon where the sun sets on the shortest day of the year. That is, it is flying to the winter solstice sunset. There are two important ideas recorded here. First, the goose marks the change in season, from fall to the beginning of winter, which is what the winter solstice signals. Second, by pointing to the west where the sun sets, bringing on the darkness of night, it refers to the fact that visible things will soon disappear into the darkness. The goose marks the change from fall to winter and from day to night.

Now that information in itself is enough to be able to proceed with some further interpretative comments. But look at where they placed the hawk. They put it right in front of the goose, flying at right angles to the long axis of the body of the goose. Then consider that the sun rises and sets, the same number of degrees south of an equinox line, a line horizontal to the equator, each day. Then on the shortest day of the year it should be clear that the hawk is flying toward the place on the horizon where the sun rises. The hawk is flying towards the place where the winter solstice sun rises, while the goose is flying towards the place where the winter solstice sun sets. Together they mark the dawn and dusk of the winter solstice. These days were extremely important for native peoples because as the days got shorter and shorter there was concern that the world might enter a period of complete darkness. Knowing that the winter solstice is the shortest day of the year and that the days lengthen from that point on, meant that there was hope that the cycles of life would continue.

Consider now that the hawk was placed in front of the goose. This is another piece of the grammar. The sun rises before the sun can set, so the hawk is placed in front of the goose to indicate that the hawk must "take off" to meet the rising sun before the goose can "take off" to meet the setting sun. In other words, there is a meaningful reason why the hawk was placed in front of the goose. One thing happens before the other in the physical world, and so too in this earth writing.

Now let us return to the second bit of information implied in the change from day to night. Animal effigies that move toward a setting sun are likely to disappear because they are going into darkness. Hawks are usually seen high in the sky, even in the winter, but geese are usually not seen in the winter at all. Geese migrate! By aligning the goose to the winter solstice sunset, they implied the concept of migration. It is true there may have been other reasons for this alignment, but we can be confident that at a minimum they had this in mind. But if you are wavering, consider the next aspect of the alignment.

Extend the line from the goose, not forward to the horizon but "backward" to the northeast. Another relationship is revealed; it connects with the three bears. The line runs approximately through the middle of the bears. Look at the bears and you will notice that the backs of the two big bears are parallel to the line of the goose. The small bear, obviously a cub, is between them. If the two adult bears were to stand up they would walk parallel to each other, but opposite the direction in which the goose is flying. When effigies are aligned together as these are, they have something in common. But when they are going in different directions, there is something different about the thing they have in common.

Now, it has probably occurred to the reader that the bears will also disappear at the time of the winter solstice. Bears hibernate. The bears and the goose both disappear. This is what they have in common. But the goose migrates while the bears hibernate, and that is what is different about what they have in common.

Now, when it is clear that there are two adults and a child, they are not describing a place of location for the clan, but rather they are making a statement about the bear "family" and by extension the Bear Clan family. Three effigy animals, two adults and a child, was a relatively common pattern around Lake Mendota. (For instance there are three such eagle effigies and again there were three such fox and thunderbird effigies on the grounds at the Mendota Mental Health Institute. There were three such water-spirit panther effigies in Governor Nelson State Park.) Having examined the two adult bears, look at the direction that the cub is walking. It is walking due east. It would walk into an equinox sunrise. They occur twice a year, in the spring and in the fall. Sometimes when we read a sentence and there is more than one possible meaning for a word, its meaning becomes clear by its context in the sentence. It is similar when "reading the mounds." When there are two possibilities, take the one that makes the most sense within the context. So is it a spring or a fall equinox sunrise? It should be clear that the bear cub is walking into the spring equinox because the parents have marked the beginning of the season that precedes spring and thus leads to spring. That is, the adult bears are in an alignment with the start of winter, indicating hibernation, and the bear cub, which in my opinion was placed purposefully between them as though it were their offspring, is aligned with the start of spring, the season of rebirth and renewal.

This becomes clearer when you realize that bear cubs are born in the den and at the time of spring when bears leave the den, they are ambulatory and ready for the world. When a pregnant female bear enters a den, she is already gestating cubs which will then be born in late January or early February. They nurse on the mother while she is hibernating in the den, and by springtime they are ready to come out. These effigy bears are sculpted to make a meaningful statement about the start of winter and to convey the ideas of both hibernation and generation. Metaphorically a mother and father go into the den and a family comes out, after a birthing process in the darkness of the winter hibernation. In reality, to be concrete, the pregnant female hibernates alone until she gives birth and then in the spring the mother and her cubs emerge from the den ready for life.

Now, to the southwest on the highest part of the hill one can see the three conical mounds. Given the almost exact similarity to the mounds cluster on the grounds at the Mendota Mental Health Institute, it is my contention that these are burial mounds for members of the Bear Clan and that the linear mounds "supplement" the conical mounds. That is, there are people and/or artifacts buried in the linear mounds that would be needed to assist the deceased Bear Clan people as they go into their spirit world. But what is the connection between the three conical mounds, the three bears and the goose? It goes something like this: first, as the adult bears entered the darkened den to hibernate, "expecting" birth to occur through which their lives will continue in their offspring, so too the deceased members of the Bear Clan have been placed in the darkness of the burial mound, "expecting" that their spirits will be born again and live on in the spirit world. As the bears leave the den to move into the new season of spring, the burial graves are only the repositories of the bodies of the Ho-Chunk, their spirits having moved on into the new "season" of the spirit world.

Second, the connection with the goose effigy mound? Just as the goose in migrating disappears but is known to continue to live because it comes back in the spring, so the spirits of the Ho-Chunk move on into their spirit world and are known to continue to live because they return in the night to communicate with their living brothers and sisters, as ghosts, apparitions, or in dreams. According to Radin and others, it was a common belief among the Ho-Chunk that the spirits of deceased relatives would appear and communicate with them in the night.

Finally, let us account for the panther mound. Just as the ancients in the Mediterranean and in China used lions to guard passages, panther mounds guarded burial grounds, the place of passage into the spirit world. As the clan that governed the lower regions, the Water-Spirits, in the form of panthers, were considered to be fierce. In the days when the old Indian trail that used to rim the lake was in use, when one was walking on that trail and came to a panther

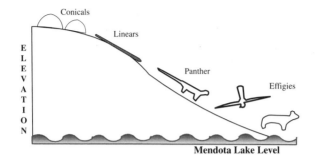

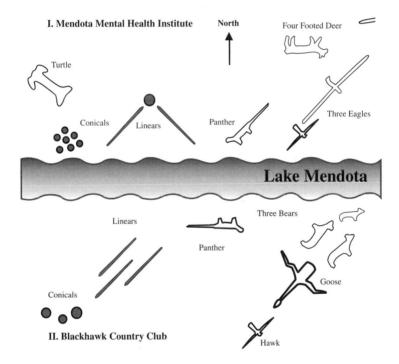

Figure 29. I. Mendota Mental Health Institute
II. Blackhawk Country Club

A schematic comparison between two groups of mounds on opposite shores of Lake Mendota. The relative positioning of Conicals—Linears—Panther—and Effigy mounds should be clear.

mound, one knew this to be a sacred area and to look for the burial site. One would see the three burials and the linears to the right and then the effigies to the left. The panther mound would say that this is sacred ground, be respectful, beware. On the hillock on the grounds of the institute, there is a large panther that has the very same function, guarding the eagle effigy mounds and the conical mounds associated with their burial. (Closer to the water and farther east, a second panther guards the boundary between the eagle effigies and the thunderbirds and foxes in the eastern cluster).

Before we finish, let us consider that we can find the very same overall construction on the north shore of Lake Mendota on the grounds of the Institute. (See Figure 29.) Earlier in this book, I describe the complex set of relationships of about fifty mounds that used to be part of one composition. About half of these mounds are still extant on the hospital grounds. While that story is beyond the telling here, what must be shared is the fact that the same minds must have conceived both constructions. In both, the conical mounds are placed on the top of the adjacent hill to the west. Long linear mounds were placed next to the conicals. Then panther mounds guard the shoreline. Finally, the effigy mounds of the clan buried in the conicals were constructed on the flat, low plain to the east, near the water.

There are effigies placed near the burials that give meaning and direction to the compositions. On the hospital grounds, a turtle effigy and a four-footed deer effigy play the role that the goose and the hawk do in this composition. But I spoke with confidence that the conical mounds on the high ground were burial mounds because the principle conical mound on the hospital grounds was excavated in 1876 and found to have three bodies in it. DeHarte reported that he found two adults and a child buried in a seated position facing west in the largest mound there. I think it is safe to conclude, since the constructions have so many key parallels, that the conicals on the top of the hill on the Blackhawk Country Club will also contain human remains, those of the Bear Clan.

But what story do these mounds tell? The whole composition tells the story of death and rebirth, using the dead of winter, the den of hibernation, and the return of the migratory. They fit together as whole gestalts in the form of effigy animals, to "concretize" in solid earth the hopeful belief that the spirits of the deceased Ho-Chunk Bear Clan are still alive, born again, into their spirit world. And for me, being able to begin to read their record has been a privilege and a gift.

Appendix B

WISDOM OF THE OAK

In the summer of 1998, a construction company building apartments on Westport Road in Westport, Wisconsin, on the north shore of Lake Mendota, made a fatal decision. They decided to bring utilities to an apartment complex by going directly across the road instead of going fifty feet west and then across. In taking the more direct approach, they cut the roots of the oldest oak tree in Dane county, killing the tree. The oak was also thought to be the second oldest oak tree in Wisconsin. When experts from the state Department of Natural Resoures verified the tree's age, and death, concerned citizens initiated a lawsuit which was resolved with the decision to engage the services of a tree sculptor, Alberto Chavez, and turn the tree into a monument.

If one looks at the tree from the road, it is easy to discern embedded in the tree itself the figure of a woman. Up to her left roosts an eagle. As one walks around the tree clockwise, one can see three otters on the northwest side, on the far north side there is the figure of a man. On the east side, to the man's left, there is a figure of a bear. If one looks carefully, one can see a thirty-foot snake that starts on the man's right side, high up, crosses down under and over, with the snake's head on the left side of the man, in front of the bear. Further, if one looks even more carefully, one can see that the man's right hand, as he reaches up, touches the tail of the snake.

I was able to discern this much just by walking around the tree several times. I then stood back and wondered what the artist meant by the construction. I was rewarded in my wondering because the artist and his wife happened by and the artist shared one interpretation of how the tree sculpture might be understood. We walked over to the north side and he pointed out how the man's right hand was sculpted touching the snake's tail. He said once the snake was touched, it became startled, so that over on the man's left the movement of the snake's head caused the bear to startle, which caused the woman to startle, which caused the eagle to startle and go into flight, which caused the otters to startle, resulting in them becoming alert. By touching the snake, the man caused a chain reaction around the tree which startled or shocked creatures that live in the water, on the surface of the earth, and in the air.

I thanked the artist for orienting me to these dynamics, and as I then walked around the tree I could see how much sense it made. He had done a very good job in portraying "startle" and given the layout of the tree's branches, he very cleverly sculpted the different figures out of the main trunk and lower branches, telling a rather dramatic story. However, it was not until I got home that I realized that there was at least one more layer to the story.

Consider that in natural cultures the snake is a symbol of earth wisdom, partly because it has the capacity to shed its skin, an annual transformation that is symbolically part of a death and rebirth process. Consider that the snake is a symbol of health in many cultures. The caduceus, that is, two coiled snakes crossing seven times, usually with the wings of Hermes across the top, is the ancient symbol of physicians, which continues to this day. (A staff with one snake coiled around it seven times from the bottom to the top represents the staff of Aeculapius, the symbolic first physician of the Greeks.) This snake then represents the ongoing healthy wisdom of the earth whose creatures live in relative harmony, going through endless cycles of death and rebirth.

It is the man, I suspect a white man, who has startled this ecological composition. Touching the snake, causing the snake to startle, parallels the actions of the construction workers, who severed the snake-like roots of the oak tree, causing the whole tree to go into shock and die. It is my opinion that the artist has stated symbolically what happened in reality, white male construction workers cut the roots of the tree in their efforts to provide "services" to an apartment complex, without any regard for the tree, thus shocking the tree and killing it. It is out of the death of the tree that the artist is trying to remind us that we can be more respectful of nature by adapting our constructions to meet the needs of nature as well as our own. If the tree had been respected as an elder in our community it would have been able to continue to teach us the lessons of old age. Let us hope that our enthusiasm for building does not severe our roots with Nature, else more than just a tree could die. We could put the whole earth at risk. The oak was about three hundred years old when it was killed. In telling the death of the tree, the artist reminds us that our culture is in danger of killing the natural world around us. But if we heed the message, then the wisdom of this elder will continue to be available to us as the oak is reborn from a living tree to a living monument.

CHAPTER NOTES

Prologue: Voices

1. The majority of the introductory quotations can be found in a favorite day-at-a-time book for those in recovery called *Touchstones: Daily Meditations for Men*, Harper Collins Publishers, New York, NY, 1987. The quotations are meant to be read at the beginning of each day in order to help keep the recovering person's thinking clear. They can also be used by families in recovery, communities in recovery, and even tribes and nations in recovery.

2. James E. Lovelock in his book *GAIA: A New Look at Life on Earth*. Oxford Press, Oxford, U.K., 1979. Describes the Greek world view in modern terms. Those not familiar with this cosmology might enjoy his views.

Chapter I. Equanimity: Living in Harmony

1. One myth of the naming of Lake Mendota is described on pp. 181-2 in *Wisconsin Lore*, by R.E. Gard and L.G. Sorden, Stanton and Lee Publishers, 1986.

2. John Neihardt in *Black Elk Speaks*, Pocket Books, New York, NY, 1959. Describes the construction and function of a Plains Indian (Sioux) sweat lodge much as it is described here. The book is rich in information about the Sioux way of life, customs, and beliefs.

3. Different tribes used varying numbers of rocks, depending on the sweat. For instance, some tribes in Wisconsin brought in seven rocks at the beginning of each round so that by the fourth round there were 28 rocks. Sometimes 21 rocks were used and at other times more than 28.

4. Joseph Brown, in his book *The Sacred Pipe*. Penquin Books, Inc., Oklahoma City, OK, 1971, has recorded Black Elk's description

of the seven rites of the Oglala Sioux. The jacket cover describes the book as "a unique account of the ancient religion of the Sioux Indians. Black Elk was the only qualified priest still alive when he gave the material in this book to Joseph Epes Brown during the latter's stay at Pine Ridge Reservation in South Dakota. Beginning with White Buffalo Cow Woman's first visit to the Sioux to give them the sacred pipe, he tells of the seven rites, which were disclosed to the Sioux through visions. The reader is led through the sun dance, the purification rite, the "keeping of the soul," and the other ceremonies, learning how the Sioux have come to terms with God, nature, and their fellow men. Shortly before his death in August 1950, Black Elk said: 'It is my prayer that through our sacred pipe, and through this book in which I shall explain what our pipe really is, peace may come to those peoples who can understand. . . . Then they will realize that we Indians know the One true God, and that we pray to Him continually'."

5. Sacred tobacco and grasses were locally grown and did not contain psychedelic or hallucinogenic substances. Peyote buttons containing mescaline and mushrooms containing psylocybin were not used in these ceremonies. "Sweating" in a sweat lodge ceremony was sometimes a prelude to ceremonies that did include the use of hallucinogens. (See Barnouw V., *Wisconsin Chippewa Myths and Tales*, University of Wisconsin Press, Madison, WI, 1977. Appendix A, "Possible Use of Amanita Muscaria." by a Chippewa Shaman).

6. In *Touch the Earth: a Self Portrait of Indian Existence*, T.C. McLuhan describes the journey of the soul of an Ojibway (or Chippewa) man to the "Happy Hunting Grounds" of his people. I repeat the following short description because it is similar to the journey of the soul of the Ho-Chunk described in Chapter VI. "When an Ojibway dies, his body is placed in a grave, generally in a sitting posture, facing the west. With the body are buried all the articles needed in life for a journey. If a man, his gun, blanket, kettle, fire steel flint and moccasins, if a woman, her moccasins, axe, portage collar, blanket and kettle. The soul is supposed to start immediately after the death of the body, on a deep beaten path, which leads westward; the first object he

comes to, in following this path, is the great Oda-e-min (Heart berry), or strawberry, which stands on the roadside like a huge rock, and from which he takes a handful and eats on his way. He travels on till he reaches a deep, rapid stream of water, over which lies the much dreaded Ko-go-gaup-o-gun, or rolling and sinking bridge; once safely over this as the traveller looks back it assumes the shape of a huge serpent swimming, twisting and untwisting its folds across the stream.

"After camping out four nights, and travelling each day through a prairie country, the soul arrives in the land of spirits, where he finds his relatives accumulated since mankind was first created; all is rejoicing, singing and dancing; they live in a beautiful country interspersed with clear lakes and streams, forests and prairies, and abounding in fruit and game in repletion—in a word, abounding in all that the red man most covets in this life, and which conduces most to his happiness. It is that kind of paradise which he only by his manner of life on this earth, is fitted to enjoy."

Chapter II. Excavation: Disturbing the Dead

1. All mounds, conical, linear, and effigy, are now protected under the Wisconsin Burial Sites Act. Since 1986 mounds must be proven not to contain a burial before they can be altered. The burden rests with the party desiring change to demonstrate that the mound is not a burial. See the Burial Sites Preservation Program, Division of Historic Preservation, The State Historical Society of Wisconsin, 816 State Street, Madison, Wisconsin 53706.

2. *National Geographic Magazine*, July, 1965, featured a cover story entitled "The Mounds Burials." The article continued the myth that a separate Indian "people" called the mound builders were responsible for constructing the mounds. This myth has now been dispelled.

3. *The Battle of Wisconsin Heights*, by C.B. Thayer is a good source of information about the dynamic events that transpired at that time.

4. Stephen D. Peet, Ph.D., published his work in a book called *The Mound Builders: Their Works and Relics*, in two volumes. The

second edition was published in 1903 by The Office of the American Antiquarian. Many of his works have been republished by the Ancient Earthworks Society.

Chapter III. Great Expectations: Surrendering Spirits

1. A book by F.W. Anderson called *Turtle Mountain Disaster*, published by Anderson in 1986, describes the Frank Slide in great geological detail. The human tragedy and reference to the Blackfoot warning are omitted.

2. After my experience with the drum dance at Fort Rae in the Northwest Territories, I wrote the following poem. It was published in *The Native Press*, the newspaper of the Indian Brotherhood of the Northwest Territories, in the spring of 1972.

The Center
Oh I am the center
the fire,
ringed by the people, who dance and who shuffle,
so tightly together around
my warm soul.

Oh I am the center
the air,
sucked in and out
by people all frenzied,
the medium of life between
thickness and thinness,
between death and life.

Oh I am the center
one person,
ringed by my brothers,
who will join and rejoin
with the rhythm of nature
as the center moves here and
moves there.

Oh I am the center
the drum,

made with a birch frame
and stretched caribou hide,
played rocking by people with
sticks from the forest,
my sound, sounding through
Being Life.

Oh I am the center
the floor
supporting the people,
who make the dance
as it weaves the many and one.

Oh I am the center
the walls,
circling the circle of
beings who round one another.
the old and the young,
the quick and the slow,
all handsome each beauty
the people who dance.

Oh I am the center
the house,
holding inside the joy of a people,
moving in circles
of friendship and love
and round me are centers
and centers and centers.

Oh I am the center
the rock,
holding the village
which dances and smiles,
between the earth and the water,
the earth and the sky,
uniting both in the tension of the
beat of the drum.

Oh I am the center
the water
I ring the village
waving back to the dancers
in ripples of rhythm
the pulsations of life.

Oh I am the center
the planet life of the forest,
of growth and recession,
of lightness and darkness,
of hope and of death.

Oh I am the center
the animal life of the forest,
the fox and the beaver,
the fly and mosquito,
the caribou and wolf,
birds of all kinds,
insects and fungus,

dogs, tame and wild,
all clothed together
in a harmony of movement
which cries joy to the world.

And I am a white man,
on the way to my center.

3. This figure is worth repeating at this point in the text to re-acquaint the reader with the layout of the mounds and hope-fully to rekindle excitement as one surveys the breadth of the complex construction.

4. I published the dream in the second newsletter of the Ancient Earthworks Society in September, 1985.

5. There is an old Greek story that describes how the gods sent messages in dreams. The gods, looking down on mortal humans, could see things that the humans could not see. After

all, humans were imperfect and not omniscient. So, from time to time the gods would decide to send useful information to the poor mortals to help them in their lives. They did this by utilizing the services of a woman called the "Mother of Dreams." Now, the task of the Mother of Dreams was to take the messages from the gods, wrap them each night in the skins of animals, and send these animals into the dreams of the mortals for whom they were intended. If the mortals were observant, they would remember the dreams they had of these animals, and symbolically remove their skins—in a form of dream interpretation—to see what the gods had to say. If a dream was not remembered, an animal would return to the Mother of Dreams. Perhaps the next night, or a few nights later, she would send the animal back into another dream with the hope that it would be remembered and the message would get through. If, after some attempts, the message was not heard, she would wrap the message in the skin of another kind of animal and try again. Her task was to send the message over and over again until it got through. While it might seem strange to the uninitiated, that an animal envoy from the gods would instruct a mortal, I was aware of this Greek model for dreams and therefore was open to listen to Nottwo.

6. In her book *The Blade and the Chalice*, Rianner Eisler offers a well researched new interpretation of the demise of the influence of the Goddess as She was replaced by the "One Male God" religions (Zeus-Yahweh and God the Father). In this process a *partnership* paradigm of human relationship was replaced by a *dominator* paradigm. Western civilization moved from a mothering respect-filled orientation to relationship to a top-down, power-oriented social structure.

7. Those interested in more information about the mounds can contact the State Historical Society of Wisconsin, or write

> Ancient Earthworks Society
> PO Box 1125
> Madison, Wisconsin 53701

Those interested in understanding Ho-Chunk customs, including further descriptions of the burial customs for the different clans, see the classic work of Paul Radin, *The Winnebago* (Ho-Chunk) *Tribe*, published by the University of Nebraska Press.

Chapter IV. The Engineer: The Eagle's View

1. Copies of survey maps of mounds groups, including the map of the Mendota mounds, may be obtained from Professor Scherz through the Department of Engineering, Engineering Hall, University of Wisconsin-Madison, Madison, WI 53706.

2. The description of Michelangelo's reconstruction of Capitoline Hill by Charles DeTolnay in the book *Michelangelo* (Princeton University Press, 1981) is as good as any.

3. There are numerous good books that describe the movement of the sun, moon, and stars, with pictures! I recommend *Pictorial Astronomy*, 6th Edition, by D. Alter, C.H. Cleminshaw, and J.G. Phillips, for a simple but comprehensive review of practical astronomy. There are also several good sources that describe the remarkable way Native Americans recorded astronomical events and coordinated their spiritual and social ceremonies with solar and lunar events. (See *In Search of Ancient Astromomies*, E.C. Kropp, 1978; *Astronomy of the Ancients*, Eds. K. Brecher and M. Feirtag, 1981; *Living the Sky,* R. Williamson, 1984; and *Early Man and the Cosmos*, E. Hardingham, 1984.)

4. Professor Scherz describes common alignments of effigy mounds in an article entitled "New Surveys of Indian Mound Layout" in the *Wisconsin Academy Review*, March 1987.

Chapter V. Education: Teaching by Example

1. Dee Brown's book, *Bury My Heart At Wounded Knee*, is still must reading for whites who doubt that the Monroe Doctrine of manifest destiny did not mean the slaughter of the Native American nations.

2. Dr. DeHarte first published his finding in a local Madison paper called the *Wisconsin Breeze*. The figure was republished by Rev. Peet in Vol. 1 of his work, *The Mounds Builders.*

3. Recent lawsuits by western Indian nations have resulted in court verdicts that direct agencies such as the Smithsonian to give back

the "bones" of thousands of natives that were removed from burial grounds and battlefields, and sent for study.

4. Mircea Eliade's book, *The Sacred and Profane: The Nature of Religion,* clarifies with good examples major mythological ideas relevant to our task. The back of the book jacket summarizes the areas covered in the book. "In a book of great originality and scholarship, a noted historian of religion traces manifestations of the sacred from primitive to modern times, in terms of space, time, nature and the cosmos, and life itself. He shows how the total human experience of the religious man compares to that of the non-religious and observes that even moderns who proclaim themselves to live in a completely profane world are still unconsciously nourished by the memory of the sacred, in camouflaged myths and degenerated rituals. *The Sacred and Profane* serves as an excellent introduction to the history of religion, but its perspective also encompasses philosophical anthropology, phenomenology, and psychology. It will be of concern to anyone seeking to discover the potential dimensions of human existence."

4. Francis Huxley's book, *The Dragon: Nature of Spirit, Spirit of Nature,* is a focused description of the role of the "snake" in world cultures. On page 7 Francis writes, "The other dragonish features of snakes consist of their living in holes in the earth, basking in the sun, swimming in water, serpentining over the ground and up trees, having a noxious breath and poisonous sting, being armored with scales at all points and, folklore has it, possessing as many ribs as there are days in the year. They also swallow their prey whole and vomit up the indigestible bones and horns in which the life of a dead animal is thought to reside, just as the righteous dead will be resurrected at the end of time from the dragon-mouth of Hell. English folklore gives this habit an Uroboric twist in the belief that a snake who eats another snake turns into a dragon, while the nature of this eating can be guessed at in the story of Tiresias, who turned into a woman when he had killed the female of two copulating snakes. He is also said to have been blinded at the sight of Athena bathing naked, which amounts to the same thing; but in compensation he was gifted with second sight and that ancient wisdom the Bible refers to as the knowledge a man has of a woman."

Chapter VI. Edgewood Retreat: Resurrecting Old Spirits

1. Gordon Brotherston has compiled a vast amount of Central American and North American original documents in a book called *Image of the New World: The American Continent Portrayed in Native Texts*. The liturgy quoted here is taken directly from the book, pp. 258-9. Radin also describes the liturgy in more detail in his book, *The Winnebago Tribe*.

2. *The Aenead* by Virgil, is a classically structured descent into the underworld and ascent to the surface to begin again, to start over, to re-birth, and in his case co-found Rome.

3. Women, too, in some religions, descend into hell to rescue and resurrect those in danger of death. In fact, in the Sutee burial of the Hindus, the wife is burned alive on the funeral pyre of her dead husband. She is specifically assigned the role of the redemption of her husband. In their theology the husband becomes sullied by work in the world and requires saving by his wife who has been given protection from the world by remaining at home. While the practice of Sutee is now unlawful, it is said that many wives went with their groom as Christ went to the cross.

4. On an Easter weekend, Dante's soul traveled to hell, rose through purgatory, and ascended to heaven to behold the beatific vision. His spiritual journey, recorded in the *Divine Comedy,* stands today as a testament to the way that symbols (hell, purgatory, heaven) open to the mystery behind the symbol. According to Joseph Campbell, when a symbol like God closes, and says he is the final God, then a religion of worship develops. But when a symbol remains open, the soul can move through it to the uncharted "Great Spirit" that lies beyond, a territory that is beyond words, beyond ideas, beyond . . . .

5. Ronald Goodman's book *Lakota Star Knowledge Studies in Lakota Stellar Theology,* describes among other things the after-death journey of the spirit among the stars. Whereas our liturgy describes a four-day journey, in this Lakota Journey the spirit (or soul) goes to the place of spirits (the Milky Way). The path the soul takes in the sky is then projected onto the earth and true

believers walk the path among the sacred places in the Black Hills in preparation for the afterdeath journey.

6. Again , DeTolnay's book *Michelangelo* offers a fascinating discussion of just those issues.

7. Rodin in fact spent time in Italy studying Michelangelo. "The Thinker," one of Rodin's most famous works, was admittedly inspired by the statue "Lorenzo" in the Medici Chapel.

8. Robert Lawlor's book, *Sacred Geometry: Philosophy and Practice* (Thames and Hudson, 1990) is an introduction to the geometry which, as the ancients taught and modern science now confirms, underlies the structure of the universe. He set out the system of number, shape, and proportion that determines the dimension and form of both man-made and natural structures, from Gothic cathedrals to flowers, from muscle to the human body.

9. Frank D. Stekel, Larry A. Johns, and James P. Scherz in "Whitewater Effigy Mounds Park: The Maples Mound Group,", published in the *Wisconsin Archeologist*, 1991, 72(1&2):118-26, pre-empted my intuition that certain mounds groups were really "open air cathedrals."

10. *The Battle of Wisconsin Heights*, by C.B. Thayer, is more than a fascinating true story. Interested readers should know that the battle site is now being restored and greater tribute paid to Blackhawk and his people. This is a small counterpoint to what Stannard called in his book, the American Holocaust.

Chapter VII. The Equinox: Polarities Balanced

1. *Seven Arrows*, by H. Storm, is a wonderful progression of animal stories that teach the lessons of the seven directions so that by the end of the journey, as one enters the seventh direction on the inward journey, "love of all my relatives" blossoms.

2. The mouse is also a common guide assigned to the south in some versions of the medicine wheel. When I first read that, I laughed. What could a mouse teach me! Whoever heard of a team called the Fighting Mice. As I listened and deflated, however, I have learned some of the lessons a mouse has to teach.

3. As an example of what is meant here, let us briefly submit to the "melody of events" in this Zuni Indian narrative of a young man's first deer hunt. His tutor is Coyote, that wise and cunning beast who so often plays the role of trickster-tutor in aboriginal American mythologies. Coyote gives the young man his hunting instructions, especially the sacred song of promise and offering, and he concludes his instructions with these words:

"Whenever you take a beast's body, give something in return. How can a man expect much without paying something? If you do not give creatures the wherewithal of changing being, how can you expect them to relish your arrows? So, whenever you slay a game creature, offer him and his like prayers-plumes—then they will feed you with their own flesh and clothe you with their own skins."

With this, they set out on the hunt, Coyote showing the young man the proper tracking techniques and outlining the strategy of attack. When the deer sights us, Coyote says, he will dart away, and I will run ahead of him to cut him off. You must do your part by singing the song of promise and offering:

Deer, deer!
Thy footprints (I see,
I following, come
Sacred favor (for thee)
I bring as I run.
Yea! Yea!

All goes well as the tracks of a huge buck are discovered and followed through the light snow cover of a canyon floor, but as Coyote and his raw pupil close in on the prey, the young hunter's excitement overcomes his training. The deer, listening nearby, hears the young voice stammer and falter in the song.

Deer, deer!
Thy footprints (I see)
I following, come;
Sacred favor (for thee)
I— I— (Oh yes!) bring as I run.
Yes! yes—oh yes!

And the buck thinks: Ah! Young hunters sometimes forget their payments of sacrifices as they do their songs; I must be off!

And with this, he turns and races up the canyon, the chagrined youth following, but the wily Coyote out in front. Again the young hunter sings the song, and this time the buck is better pleased, but still doubtful, and he flees again before his tracker. He stops again farther on and hears the song of offering drifting up to him. "Ha!" he thinks. "I should die contented, could I know that he would make payment—but who knows?"

Alarmed by his own doubt, he springs away once again. Now for the final time the words of the song are borne to him, but this time, turning to flee, he is cut off by Coyote. Caught between two tormentors, the buck charges the trailing hunter whose fright-sent, ill-aimed arrow shatters its shaft harmlessly against the boss of the antlers. Like the first shot, the charge miscarries, and the buck wheels again against the hunter. This time the young man is equal to his task, and his arrow is buried to its very feathers in the massive breast of the charging beast. The buck staggers, falls, struggles to rise again as Coyote shouts to the young man to shoot again. But the novitiate can remember only that he has not yet fulfilled the next step of the ritual, which is to embrace the fallen prey, breathe his breath, and say, "Thanks, father, this day have I drunken your sacred wind of life." Now the young man dodges between the frantically thrusting antlers and places his face against that of the buck, breathing its life's breath, covered with its life's blood, until finally the prey relaxes and relinquishes to him.

Coyote is joyous, for such fortune is a sign that the Beings of the Game will befriend this hunter forever. After instructing him further in the necessary sacrificial offerings to be made at the site of the killing, Coyote reminds the hunter of their significance.

Thou receivest flesh wherewith to add unto thy own flesh. For this thou shalt always confer in return that which giveth new life to the hearts of slain creatures.

And now the man can hunt alone.

The narrative's intentions are clear and large. It inculcates the lesson of humility before nature and of gratitude for what nature may choose to grant. It teaches also the lesson of trust in oneself, a trust founded on both the proper observances of the hunting rituals and on a sense of symbiosis as a law that embraces both hunter and hunted. And, through the fiction of the language of the animals and the converse between them and the human being, it teaches the interconnectedness of all things. The Trickster Cycle of the Ho-Chunk was described by Radin and interpreted by Carl Jung.

4. Judith Gold's Editorial, "The Intolerance of Aloneness" in The *American Journal of Psychiatry*, June, 1996, is a current statement by a psychiatrist of the psychological impact of prolonged "loneliness."

5. Jill Purce has written an interesting book called the *Mystic Spiral: Journey of the Soul,* which describes the pervasive presence and influence of the spiral form in primary cultures. It is not surprising that this form is also present in some of the mounds' constructions.

6. Rites of passage such as the vision quest at puberty or entrance into the lodge were also a time of "learning" as M. Eliade says on p. 193 of the *Sacred and the Profane*, "We may note again that the rites for entrance into a secret society correspond in every respect to puberty/initiations—seclusion, initiatory ordeals and torture, death and resurrection, bestowel of a new name, introduction in a secret language and so on."

7. Michael Harner, *The Way of the Shaman*, Harper & Row, San Francisco, California, 1990.

Chapter VIII. The Great Eagle: The Return of the Executive

1. Lewis surveyed more than 30,000 mounds in over 500 different locations. They all tell stories. Unfortunately most have been destroyed. With the help of the Native Americans the stories will become known. It will be thanks to explorer-surveyors like Peet and Lewis that this written legacy will have been preserved.

2. Phelps announced his plan on September 3, 1991.

3. Masters and Houston described four levels of conscious experience in their book *Varieties of LSD Experience.*

4. On page 3 of his book *Lakota Star Knowledge*, Goodman makes the same point. Here it is in his words. "The stories of the Lakota Oral Tradition are sacred literature. Therefore, they must, like other scriptures, be understood on four levels of consciousness. These levels correspond, the Lakota say, to our physical, emotional, intellectual, and spiritual natures, and these are related to the unfolding of the four stages of life: childhood, youth, adulthood, and old age. The first three levels of understanding can come eventually to any earnest seeker, as he or she grows and matures. But the spirits alone can give us the last and highest comprehension. All four levels are true and those four truths are one truth. The medicine men say that how deeply each of us understands the stories tells us about the level we have attained in our own lives. Similar levels when reading Jewish and Christian scriptures have traditionally been called: (1) literal, (2) allegorical, (3) moral/philosophical and (4) anagogical."

5. *American Holocaust,* subtitled *Columbus and the Conquest of the New World,* by D.E. Stannard, documents the destruction of an estimated one hundred million north and central American "Indians" by starvation, overwork, mass killings and infectious disease. The numbers, that is the current updated estimates of the population in the Americas, are much greater than previously thought (less than 10,000,000).

6. *Letters from North America*, by Father A. Silvy, S.J., gives a Jesuit's view of life with the Iroqouis in the early seventeenth century. It is relevant to us because it describes their lifestyle before it was interrupted by Europeans who were trying to "convert" them.

Chapter IX. The Ghost Eagle: The Spirit Returns

1. In "Stories of Natural Wisdom," published in the second *Mythos Journal*, I tell four stories that progress from my mother's winter story through the Frank Slide to the Middleton Turtle. I also tell a fourth story of how Anna Halprin and friends used the Indian myth of a sleeping maiden in Mt. Tamalpais, to unlock the psychic energy held in the mountain to make the mountain safe for women and men. I called the story the "Rape-Murder and the Sleeping Princess."

Over a period of eighteen months, from late 1979 to early 1981, five women were sexually assaulted and murdered while jogging on Mount Tamalpais, in Marin County, California. While the police worked to apprehend the criminal(s), they were forced to close the mountain because of the ongoing danger. The rape-murders and the closing of the mountain both frightened and enraged local residents. At the time Anna Halprin, a local resident, was working with a group of people who were searching for ways to bring the meaning of Indian myths to life. They were aware that the Miwok, the indigenous Indians, told a story of an Indian Princess asleep in Tamalpais Mountain who would awaken when men and women could live in harmony. Since Anna was a teacher of modern dance, she decided to score a dance based on the rape-murders and the Miwok Indian myth. By joining the energy aroused by the rape-murders to the structure of the myth, they hoped to rouse the sleeping maiden and bring safety to women. They decided to perform the dance on the Mountain so that the community could reclaim it for its people. The dance began in the Mill Valley community center. The dancers then drove to the top of Mount Tamalpais and danced down the Mountain. Two days after the dance, the police received a telephone call that resulted in the arrest of a suspect. The rape-murders stopped and the suspect was ultimately convicted (Halprin).

The association between the dance and the capture of the criminal came to the attention of a 106-year-old Huichol Indian shaman who was in San Francisco at the time. He called Anna and told her that to ensure that the Mountain would remain safe, she would need to repeat the dance annually for five years. (The criminal was arrested two days after the first dance and was convicted four years and nine months later, after facing other charges in Los Angeles in the intervening years.) This resulted in the annual "circle the mountain dances." Because local interest was high and the dances seemed to provide a significant mode of ritual expression, the dances have been expanded and are now called "circle the earth dances." If the princess sleeping in the mountain could be reawakened by the conscious efforts of an outraged community to make the mountain safe, perhaps the feminine sleeping in patriarchal societies can be brought to life so that the earth will become a safe place for all life.

2. The big city-little city battle between Madison and Middleton was depicted as a win for Middleton in the local press. C. Segall described the final round in the *Wisconsin State Journal* (May 31, 1989) in an article with the headline "Middleton Wins Street Fight."

Epilogue: White Buffalo Calf Woman

1. Four years later, the Heider Farm, and the White Buffalo, are still a site of pilgrimage for Native Americans and other natural people. Harry White Horse, a Madison artist, has crafted a larger than life-size sculpture of Miracle, the white buffalo calf. He presented it to the Heiders and to Miracle the calf, on the calf's second birthday. (*Wisconsin State Journal,* August 20, 1996)

Appendix A: The Blackhawk Mounds and New Beginnings

1. Lenzendorf, D., *Effigy Mounds: A Guide to Effigy Mounds National Monument.* Eastern National, Fort Washingtgon, PA, 2000.

2. Radin, P., *The Winnebago Tribe*, University of Nebraska Press, Lincoln, 1923.

3. *Wisconsin's Past and Present: A Historical Atlas*, The Wisconsin Cartographers' Guild, University of Wisconsin Press, Madison, 1998.

4. *National Geographic Magazine*, July, 1965.

5. Markwardt, L. J., *Blackhawk Indian Mounds on the National Register of Historic Places,* 1979.

6. Markwardt, L. J., *The Blackhawk Country Club and Its Historic Indian Heritage,* American Revolution Bicentennial, 1776-1976.

The photograph on the cover depicts the Eagle from the Westport Oak Tree Sculpture, by Alberto Chavez, 1998.